GOD'S OVERCOMERS

A Record of the Third Overcomer Conference

WATCHMAN NEE

Living Stream Ministry
Anaheim, California • www.lsm.org

July 1999

ISBN: 0-7363-0433-9
Library of Congress Catalog Card Number: 99-73343

Published by

Living Stream Ministry
2431 W. La Palma Ave., Anaheim, CA 92801 U.S.A.
P. O. Box 2121, Anaheim, CA 92814 U.S.A.

Printed in the United States of America

CONTENTS

PREFACE

A WORD OF EXPLANATION CONCERNING THE THIRD OVERCOMER CONFERENCE

Between 1928 and 1934, Brother Watchman Nee conducted four Overcomer Conferences. The subjects of these conferences were on "God's Central Messages." The first conference was held in February 1928 on the subject: "God's Eternal Purpose and the Victory of Christ." The second conference was held in October 1931 on the subject: "The Covenant of God and the Wisdom of God." The third conference was held in January 1934 on the subjects: "Christ as the Centrality and Universality of God" and "God's Overcomers." The fourth conference was held in October of the same year on the subjects: "The Life of Abraham" and "Spiritual Warfare." Except for the fourth conference, which was held in Hangchow, all the other conferences were in Shanghai.

The messages of the Third Overcomer Conference were first published in three issues of the magazine *The Present Testimony,* published by Watchman Nee.

In this present edition, Chapter 1, entitled "Preparation Messages of the Third Overcomer Conference," presents short messages given in the first two days of the conference, January 22 and 23, 1934. Chapters 2 and 3, entitled "God's Center or The Centrality and Universality of Christ" and "The Overcomer of God," present the main parts of the conference messages. (The chapter on "The Overcomer of God" has been additionally supplemented with a section, "The Experience of the Overcomers" taken from Brother Weigh Kwang-hsi's notes.) Two of the outlines presented in Chapter 1 were published in more polished form later; thus, "Ministering to the House or to God?" and "A Shallow Life," are included as Chapters 4 and 6. A separate message which was not part of the Third Overcomer Conference, "Having Been Made Dead to the Law," is included in this volume as Chapter 5 to retain the original order of the messages as they appeared in *The Present Testimony*.

Chapters 7 and 8, "What Are We?" and "Questions Related to the Workers," were translated from notes by Brother Weigh Kwang-hsi. These messages were released during and after the same conference. "What Are We?" points out the testimony that God is after, based on the history of the recovery of the truth. "Questions Related to the Workers" covers the nature of the work and its relationship with the church. Although these messages were not published in *The Present Testimony,* we have included them here with the messages released during this period.

The nature and burden of this conference can be found in Watchman Nee's note, "A Letter Concerning the Third Overcomer Conference." A more detailed report of the conference can be found in Issue No. 4 of *Collection of Newsletters* in Set Two of *The Collected Works.*

A LETTER CONCERNING

THE THIRD OVERCOMER CONFERENCE

"Jesus is Lord!" (1 Cor. 12:3).

We have previously held two conferences of the same nature, one in February of 1928 and one in October of 1931. The conference held in November of last year was of a different nature, and for that reason we consider the upcoming conference to be the third overcomer conference.

I want all the brothers to understand the nature of this type of conference; no attention will be paid to the less significant matters of the Bible. What we want to see in the Holy Spirit is Christ and Him crucified. Matters such as prophecy, church organization, Scripture exposition, types, baptism, laying on of hands, speaking in tongues, miracles, and a hundred other questions have their proper place. As Christians we should not deny them their proper place. However, these are neither the center of the Scriptures nor the center of the life of the Holy Spirit. God has only one center, which is Christ—Christ and Him crucified. Our annual conferences of this nature are to bring us back to this center. Therefore, we are reluctant to mention any minor matters in these conferences. Rather, we would emphasize only the central point which God Himself stressed.

Many people often ask us why *The Present Testimony* does not print some of the articles similar to those in the previous magazine, *The Christian*. However, they do not realize that *The Present Testimony* only delivers the central message of God. Many of the gospel messages, interpretations of prophecy, Bible expositions, and answers to questions are not God's center. It is a pity that many believers treasure our writings on these side issues, but neglect the central message. We are not saying that the other subjects are useless; they do have their place. However, they are not the center. If a person has not laid hold of God's center, all these truths will only be doctrines to him and will not give him any help. Knowing God in His center, and living in the center is victory, holiness, and glory. Everything else follows afterward.

In our conference this time, as before, we wish to lay stress on the central message. After much prayer I feel the theme which the Lord has given me for this conference is "God's Overcomers." Everything in the conference will focus on this center. Since the dates are now set, I ask all the brothers to pray more for this conference. Unlike the conference in 1928, our conferences in 1931 and 1932 were both lacking in prayer. Consequently, we saw no obvious blessing in those meetings. We should, therefore, ask God for a burden to pray and for a spirit of prayer. We need to pray and pray fervently. Perhaps we even have to fast and pray. However, we must pray in the Holy Spirit! Whether or not God will bless us depends upon our prayer.

Finally, in this conference, our hope is to meet Christ, to receive light and revelation from heaven, and to be filled with the life that is unknown to ordinary people. We do not intend to pay attention to the many minor, outward matters. "To know Him" (Phil. 3:10)—this is what we seek.

Your brother,
Watchman Nee
December 13, 1933

1

PREPARATION MESSAGES
OF THE THIRD OVERCOMER CONFERENCE

"They shall come near to Me to minister to Me; and they shall stand before Me to present to Me the fat and the blood, declares the Lord Jehovah."
Ezekiel 44:15b

"I will be like the dew to Israel;
He will bud like the lily
And will send forth his roots like the trees of Lebanon."
Hosea 14:5

THE PURSUIT OF THOSE WHO SERVE THE LORD

Scripture Reading:
Ezekiel 44:9-26, 28, 31; Luke 17:7-10
("minister" in Ezek. 44:11 can be translated "serve")

The Difference between Working for the Lord and Serving the Lord

The Lord wants us to serve Him more than He wants us to work for Him. Ministering to the house and serving before the Lord's table are different things. Working for the Lord and serving the Lord are different things. Tilling the field and shepherding the flock are different from serving in the presence of the master.

What the sons of Levi did was different from what the sons of Zadok did. The Levites ministered to the house in the outer court; they killed the sacrifices before the people and ministered on their behalf. The sons of Zadok ministered to the Lord's table within the Holy Place and served the Lord by offering the fat and the blood. The work of the Levites in the outer court was apparent. The work of the priests in the Holy Place was hidden. In the outer court one ministered to the people. In the Holy Place one ministered to the Lord. The ministry in the outer court appears to be serving the Lord. Actually, it is very different from serving the Lord in the house.

Many people like to exercise their muscles in the outer court. They like to help others move and kill the sacrifices, but they do not like to serve the Lord in the Holy Place. Many people like to run around in an outward way; they like to save sinners, edify the believers, and serve the brothers. But the Lord wants us to pursue a service to Him.

God's work has its interests and attractions. The attractions of the flesh do exist within God's work. Many people love to run around and work because this is what their flesh is inclined to do. Outwardly, they are saving sinners and serving the brothers. Actually, they are serving their own flesh and their own pleasures. One believer who has passed the veil and who is on the other side of the veil prayed after reading Ezekiel 44: "Lord, may I minister unto You, rather than unto the house!"

Ministering to the Lord in the Holy Place

"They shall come near to Me to minister to Me" (Ezek. 44:15). In the outer court one comes near to the people. In the Holy Place one comes near to the Lord. It is possible to follow the Lord "at a distance" (Matt. 26:58), but it is not possible to minister to the Lord at a distance. In order to minister to the Lord, one has to come near to Him. The prayer that brings one near to the Lord gives him strength. It also requires that he exercise his strength.

"And they shall stand before Me" (Ezek. 44:15). Not only must one come near to the Lord, but he must also stand before Him. Many people cannot stand and wait. To stand is to wait for an order. All those who cannot stand and wait before the Lord cannot minister to Him. We have two kinds of sins. One is to receive a command and not obey it; this is rebellion. The other is to have no command and yet do something; this is presumption (Psa. 19:13). It is not a matter of good or bad but of having or not having God's command. Good things can damage the believers very much; they are a great enemy to God's will. In the outer court one takes orders from the offerers of sacrifices. In the Holy Place one takes orders from God.

"To present to Me the fat and the blood" (Ezek. 44:15). God's righteousness and holiness fill the Holy Place, and His glory fills the Holy of Holies. The blood is for God's righteousness and holiness, while the fat is for God's glory. Glory is God Himself. Holiness is God's nature, while righteousness is God's procedure, His way. The blood is there for the forgiveness of sins; it satisfies God's righteousness and holiness, and it enables us to come to God. The fat is to satisfy God Himself. The blood deals with the old creation, while the fat is for the new creation. When the Lord poured out His blood, it meant that He poured out all His natural life. Today the Lord has flesh and bones (Luke 24:39) but no blood. He does not have a drop of blood. Every day we have to learn to deny our natural life before the Lord; this is the aspect of the blood. At the same time, we have to offer up the resurrection life; this is the aspect of the fat (Rom. 6:13).

"It is they who will enter My sanctuary" (Ezek. 44:16). To be in the sanctuary is to be in the presence of the Lord. We are very afraid of being in the sanctuary because if we remain in the sanctuary it is easy to be misunderstood, slandered, and criticized. But we should dwell in the house of the Lord. We are not narrow; our hearts are broad and ambitious. Paul said in his Epistles that he was determined to be well pleasing to the Lord (2 Cor. 5:9). We have to pursue ministering to the Lord rather than to the house.

"No wool will come upon them" (Ezek. 44:17). "They shall

not gird themselves with anything that causes sweat" (v. 18). Sweat is a condition of the curse (Gen. 3:19). To sweat is to be without the Lord's blessing and to labor by the flesh. One can sweat when he kills the bulls and the goats in the outer court. But he cannot sweat when he is ministering to the Lord in the Holy Place. One can exert spiritual strength before the Lord, but he must not sweat. Committees, discussions, and propagandas all belong to the realm of sweating. Spiritual work touches God alone, while fleshly work touches men alone. The more spiritual a work is, the more inward it is. But the work of the flesh is all outward.

God did not command all the Levites to minister to Him in the Holy Place. He only ordered the sons of Zadok to minister to Him in the Holy Place. God invites men to minister to Him in His Holy Place. He wants men to preserve His Holy Place, shine out from there, and separate the holy things from the common things, and the clean things from the unclean things. Acts 13:1-3 tells us when "they were ministering to the Lord and fasting," the Holy Spirit sent them out on their missionary work abroad. Our work abroad should start with our ministering to the Lord. The Lord is after drafted workers, not volunteer workers. Hebrews emphasizes two things: our ministering to God within the veil and our suffering the reproach of the Lord without the camp.

Ministering to Him after Working

In Luke 17:7-10, "plowing" is preaching of the gospel, while "tending sheep" is caring for the believers. To "serve me" means that one has to minister to the Lord even after he has worked. To "eat and drink" is to remember and to enjoy the fruit of our work; we must first allow the Lord to "eat and drink" before we enjoy eating and drinking. The result of our work should first satisfy the Lord's heart before it satisfies our heart. After we have worked, we should not eat, drink, and enjoy; rather, we should say, "We are unprofitable slaves." "Gird yourself and serve me" means that after one has worked, he should still be on the alert to minister to the Lord. May we pursue a ministry to the Lord. The work in the field is not as good as the ministry in the house, and the field and the sheep are not as good as the Lord Himself. ❧

(Morning, January 22, 1934)

THE HIDDEN LIFE

Scripture Reading:
Song of Songs 4:12; Hosea 14:5-7; Mark 4:5-6, 16-17

A Shallow Life

Mark 4 speaks of the condition of man's heart and how it receives the word. It does not apply only to sinners hearing the gospel, but also to believers receiving the word of edification.

What is the kind of life that pleases the Lord and lasts long? Why have some failed or turned back halfway? Why are there so few who have followed the Lord all the way? Some people are very willing at the beginning to give up everything to consecrate themselves fully to the Lord and to follow Him. But when they encounter something along the way which is contrary to their will, they decide not to follow the Lord anymore. If you have never been dealt with by the Lord or have not fully consecrated yourself, the day will come when the Lord will take you to a place where you do not want to go, and you will reject His choice. The price will be too high for you, and you will find that you cannot pay it. This is why you must be dealt with by the Lord until you are fully consecrated to take up the cross to follow Him all the way. All the ones who turned back or failed halfway are the ones with the shallow ground.

"It sprang up" (Mark 4:5). This refers to those who have

received the word and made a start outwardly. However, the result is not good because there is no root; when the sun rises, it is scorched and withers. Every word brings with it affliction and persecution. God prepares circumstances behind every word of His to test if we have received His word properly. The sun is the ultimate sign of the Lord's love. The cross not only separates the sinners as to who are saved and who are perishing; it also separates the believers as to who are the overcoming ones and who are the defeated ones. Spiritual dryness comes because one argues with God and defeats Him by allowing himself to win. Miss Barber once said, "All the bread that is in the Lord's hand, He will surely break." Many times we put ourselves in the Lord's hand, while at the same time we pray privately, "Please do not break me!"

Why do the ones on the rocky place, who spring up quickly, also wither quickly? First, they have "no depth of earth" (v. 5). All those who live in their environment or their emotions are those who are in shallow earth. Those who are deep live above their circumstances; they deny their feelings and live in the Lord. They receive God's supply, support, and power beyond their environments. Second, they are without root. Those who have life in an outward way are like the plant stalk, but those with life in an inward way are like the roots. Roots denote a hidden and secret life. The Lord says that we have to shut the door and pray in secret (Matt. 6:6). God will *see* us, not *hear* us, in secret. The most dangerous life is one that is only before men. The safest life is one that is before God. Those who have been dealt with by God in secret, who have deep roots, will overcome all affliction and persecution. Third, there are rocks under the earth. On the surface, one place is the same as all other places. But underneath, it is different; there are rocks underneath. (1) The rocks are the hardened heart (Heb. 3:15). If we want to hear the Lord's word, we cannot harden our hearts or have our own prejudices. Those whose self is still hidden within them and who have not been broken by the Lord cannot have deep roots. (2) The rocks are also hidden sins. As long as these sins have not been removed, the roots cannot go down deep. Only those who tremble at God's word and are feeble as little children will grow. The Lord has to smash all the hardened hearts and human prejudices. He can ride on a colt that has never been sat on before, and he can deal with those who have never obeyed Him before.

A Life in the Depth

Hosea 14:5-7 mentions Lebanon three times: (1) the lily in contrast to Lebanon, (2) the olive tree in contrast to Lebanon, and (3) the vine in contrast to Lebanon. In the whole world, the trees with the deepest roots are the cedars of Lebanon. We should go down and take root in the depths; we should direct our growth to the depths.

Although the lily looks pretty, it grows in the wilderness. We are the lily in the valley, not in the pot. We are not cared for by the gardener but by God. We do not receive any supply from men but from God alone. The rain from heaven is watering us, and we are sustained by God.

The beauty of the olive tree is not in its flower but in the oil-bearing fruit. We should bring forth the fruit of the Spirit.

The flower of the vine is very small. Before a man can discover it, it has turned into grapes. The flowers are for fruit-bearing, not for beauty.

A Hidden Life

The Song of Solomon 4:12 mentions "a garden enclosed." It is a garden, not a park. It is enclosed, not open. Within the garden are fruits and flowers. The things we have which are for the Lord alone should be enclosed. All the things we have within us should be for the Lord alone. As such, they should be enclosed.

"A spring shut up, a fountain sealed." In the Chinese Union Version, *spring* is translated *well.* A well is something man-made, while a fountain is something natural. A well is there to serve man, while a fountain is there to receive from God. The well is directed toward men, while a fountain is directed toward God. Although we are directed toward men and are for men's use, we are "shut up," and we wait for the Lord to open us and use us. Although we are directed toward God and are here to receive from God, we are "sealed." We should be closed to both God and men. We should allow the cross to do a deeper work in us and deal with our self, so that we can have a deeper life. We should maintain a hidden life before God. ❦

(Afternoon, January 22)

THE CONDITIONS FOR SPIRITUAL GROWTH

Scripture Reading:
2 Kings 4:1-6; Matthew 5:6; Luke 1:53

The Reason for Not Growing

The only reasons for the believers' failures and lack of growth before God are (1) not knowing themselves and (2) not knowing the fullness of the Lord. At a Keswick Convention, one anonymous Christian said that all the failures of believers are from these two reasons.

The Only Condition for Growth

The only condition for God's blessing, spiritual growth, or the experience of the fullness of the Lord is to be empty. We have to constantly realize our own fullness, and we should also constantly empty ourselves of our own fullness. We should constantly empty ourselves. Only those who are hungry will be filled with good things (Luke 1:53). All God's spiritual grace is only for the hungry ones.

The order of the Holy Spirit's work in us is first to create a desire in our heart so that we become dissatisfied with our present life. The beginning of regression is satisfaction, and the beginning of progress is dissatisfaction. The Holy Spirit first does the work of emptying and then the work of filling. God empties us in order to fill us. The emptying is God's means, while the filling is His goal. In order to empty us, the Holy Spirit puts us against a wall and allows us to encounter crises. All the difficulties are arranged by the Holy Spirit for the purpose of making us pursue in a deeper way. The victory at Jericho cannot be relied upon for the battle at Ai. We cannot apply the big victory of yesterday to even the small battle of today. Past experiences cannot meet present needs. God never asks us to eat the manna of yesterday. Thank God that we have crises! Through the Holy Spirit, God has created crises for us in our environment and in our lives. He allows us to fail when we try to meet present crises with past experiences. The failure creates a need and a fresh desire in us. Faith never copies the things of the past. We cannot imitate the works of faith of the believers in the past; we can only imitate their faith. Since the disciples saw the Lord feeding the five thousand with the five loaves, and the four thousand with the seven loaves, they should have known further that He could fill them even if there were no loaves. They did not know the Lord in a deeper way. This was why they said, "It is because we did not take bread" (Matt. 16:7). God arranges the environment for us that we might know the Lord more, know ourselves more, and know the vanity of the self. He allows us to fail so that we could realize our emptiness and uselessness. Our person has already been nullified by God on the cross.

The Way to Be Filled

Second Kings 4:1-6 says, "Now a certain woman from among the wives of the sons of the prophets cried out to Elisha, saying, Your servant my husband is dead, and you know that your servant feared Jehovah. And the creditor has come to take my two children to himself as servants. And Elisha said to her, What shall I do for you? Tell me, what do you have in your house? And she said, Your servant has nothing at all in the house, except a jar of oil. And he said, Go and borrow vessels outside, from all your neighbors, empty vessels, and not just a few. Then go in and shut the door behind you and your sons, and pour out into all those vessels; and each one you fill set aside. So she went away from him and shut the door behind herself and her sons; and they brought the vessels to her, and she poured out into them. And when she had filled the vessels, she said to her son, Bring me another vessel. But he said to her, There is no other vessel. And the oil stopped."

Preparing the Empty Vessels

The woman became a debtor because of the poverty of her husband. But she had a jar of oil. This jar of oil was the basic ingredient. It was this jar of oil that allowed her to pay her debt and that supplied her daily needs. She needed empty vessels. Elisha ordered her to prepare empty vessels, and not a few. Through Adam we have become poor. But praise the Lord, we have the Holy Spirit. What is lacking are empty spots for the Spirit to fill. The fact is not that we cannot be filled, but that we do not have the empty spots for the Holy Spirit to work into. The Holy Spirit will only fill the empty spots. For spiritual progress we must be continually empty to be continually filled. It is not to be emptied once and then remain full forever. Time after time we need further emptying and further filling.

Shutting the Door

One has to deal with the Holy Spirit secretly in the hidden place. The flesh has to be locked outside, and the Holy Spirit locked inside. Whenever one encounters problems, he has to go to the hidden place to deal with the Holy Spirit. When we deal with the Spirit, the problems in our lives are solved.

The Oil Ceases When There Are No More Empty Vessels

The oil ceased because there were no more empty vessels. The filling stops when there is no more emptiness. If there is unlimited emptiness, there will be unlimited filling. Esau was the first self-satisfied person. In the end he became an empty person. We should continually empty ourselves, instead of emptying ourselves just once. We should continually empty ourselves so that we can be continually filled. We are responsible for the emptying, and the Holy Spirit is responsible for the filling. ❀

(Morning, January 23)

THE PRAYER THAT COOPERATES WITH GOD

Scripture Reading:
Isaiah 62:6; Ezekiel 36:37; Philemon 14

The Principle of God's Work

God works along certain lines and according to certain principles. He does not do things haphazardly or carelessly. He would rather not work than have work that is done contrary to His principle. If we want to receive His blessings, we have to fulfill the conditions for Him to bless.

God transcends all principles and rules. Yet He likes to lay down principles for His work so that both He and man would abide by these ordained principles. God's principle is God's will.

God never works by Himself. He always puts His desire in His children's heart so that they would pray for it. Mr. Evan Roberts said that the order of all God's works is:

(1) God has a desire.

(2) Through the Holy Spirit, He puts this desire within His children's hearts.

(3) God's children turn this desire back to God through prayer.

(4) God accomplishes this desire.

The whole thing begins with God's desire. Through the Holy Spirit, God puts this desire in the hearts of His children so that they will know what is His heart's desire. His children then turn this desire into prayer and send it back to God. As a result, He works to accomplish that which is according to His desire.

Ezekiel 36:37 says, "Thus says the Lord Jehovah, Moreover for this I will be inquired of by the house of Israel to do it for them; I will increase them with men like a flock."

(1) God ordained that the number in the house of Israel be increased. This is God's decision and what He will do. It is the first point and also the fourth point mentioned earlier.

(2) But God still has to be inquired of by the house of Israel. Although God made the decision to increase the number of the house of Israel, He could only accomplish it after He had been inquired of by the house of Israel. This is the principle of God's work. God only has His will; He does not work. He must wait until His children inquire of Him and then He will work. God is not trying to hold back on any of His work. He is waiting for His children to inquire of Him before He will work. He is willing to put Himself under the authority of and be limited by His children's prayer. If they do not pray, He cannot work. For over twenty-five hundred years, God has not increased the number of the house of Israel because no one has inquired this of Him.

Isaiah 62:6 says, "Upon Your walls, O Jerusalem, / I have appointed watchmen; / All day and all night / They will never keep silent. / You who remind Jehovah, / Do not be dumb."

(1) God has ordained that Jerusalem would be a praise in the earth. This is God's desire.

(2) For this He has set watchmen to cry out to Him. He told them not to hold their peace and to give Him no rest. We should pray continually and not rest until God accomplishes what He has ordained. The carrying out of God's will is fully determined by our prayer.

Philemon 14 says, "But without your mind I did not want to do anything, that your goodness would not be as of necessity, but voluntary."

Paul represents God, and Philemon represents us. Paul would not do anything without knowing Philemon's mind. God will not do anything without knowing our mind. His will is limited by us.

Prayer Being the Tracks of God's Will

Mr. Gordon Watts once said that God's will is like a locomotive, while our prayers are like the tracks. The locomotive is powerful, but it can only run on the tracks. God's will is powerful, but it needs our prayer as the tracks before His will can be done. God would not work alone; He has to wait for His children's will to agree with His will before He will work. There are three wills in the universe: God's will, man's will, and Satan's will. God does not remove Satan's will by Himself. He desires that man's will become one with His will, to deal with Satan's will. A spiritual prayer is an utterance of God's will. How useless is a prayer that merely utters one's own will! Our prayer cannot change God's will; it merely expresses His will. God is the initiator of everything; we are merely the channel through which His will can flow. God ordains, and we obey. He initiates, and we agree in prayer. We cannot force God to do what He does not want to do, but we can stop Him from doing what He does want to do. When God's will is turned into our prayer, He will begin working. Every revival comes from prayer. Our prayer cannot change God's will; it only speaks out His will. No one can direct God's will, and no one can make Him do what He does not want to do. However, what He does want to do can be limited by man's prayer. Although Pentecost was prophesied by God in the book of Joel, there had to be the prayer of the one hundred and twenty before He could accomplish this. God's will reaches only as far as our prayers have reached. Therefore, the more thorough our prayers are, the more the will of God will be accomplished, and Satan's deceptions will not be able to come in. We should cast a net of prayer "by means of all prayer and petition, praying at every time" (Eph. 6:18), so that God's will can prevail in all areas, and Satan will not find one crack through which to come in. In our prayer we should pay attention to three things: (1) to whom we are praying, (2) for whom we are praying, and (3) against whom we are praying. All our prayers should fulfill God's will, afford others a profit, and inflict Satan with a loss.

(Afternoon, January 23)

2

GOD'S CENTER
OR
THE CENTRALITY AND UNIVERSALITY OF GOD

"...Christ is all and in all."
Colossians 3:11

"And He is the Head of the Body, the church;
He is the beginning, the Firstborn from the dead,
that He Himself might have the first place in all things."
Colossians 1:18

Scripture Reading:
Colossians 3:11; 1:18; 2:2; 2 Corinthians 4:5

THE MEANING OF THE CENTER

Why are there all things? Why are there angels? Why are there human beings? Has God created these things without a purpose, or are they a part of God's plan?

Why did God choose man, commission the prophets, send the Savior, give us the Holy Spirit, set up the church, and establish the kingdom? Why would God want to spread the gospel to the uttermost part of the earth and save sinners? Why do we have to save sinners and edify the believers?

Some have considered baptism, speaking in tongues, forsaking the denominations, holiness, the keeping of the Sabbath, or other things as the center. But what is God's center?

God's work is with a goal. What is the goal of our work? We must first have a goal in our vision and then have a goal in our work. If we do not see God's center, our work will not have any goal.

God's truths are all systematic and interrelated. There is a center to God's truths, and everything else is auxiliary.

Some have determined the center of their work by basing it on their own inclinations and the need around them. But our center should be according to God's predestination and His need.

What is God's center? What is God's consistent truth? What is the one line in God's truth?

Who is the Lord Jesus? We all say that He is our Savior, but very few people can say as Peter did, that He is the Christ of God.

The center of God's truths is Christ. God's center is Christ. "The mystery of God, Christ" (Col. 2:2). A mystery is something hidden in God's heart. God never told anyone why He created all things and why He created man. Hence, it was a mystery. Later He revealed this mystery to Paul and charged him to speak it out. This mystery is Christ.

The Lord Jesus is the Son of God; He is also the Christ of God. When the Lord was born, an angel told Mary that He is the Son of God (Luke 1:35), but the angels told the shepherds that He is Christ the Lord (Luke 2:11). Peter acknowledged Him both as the Christ and as the Son of God (Matt. 16:16). When the Lord resurrected, He was designated the Son of God (Rom. 1:4). Through His resurrection, God also made Him both Lord and Christ (Acts 2:36). A man receives life by believing that He is the Christ and the Son of God (John 20:31). In Himself, as far as His person is concerned, the Lord is the Son of God. In God's plan, according to His work, He was anointed by God and is, therefore, the Christ of God. He is the Son of God from eternity to eternity. He is the Christ since the beginning of God's plan. God's goal is for His Son to have "the first place in all things" (Col. 1:18). God's plan is focused on Christ. "Christ is all and in all" (Col. 3:11).

God created all things, and He created man for the purpose of expressing Christ's glory. Today believers express only a little of Christ. In the future all things will express Christ; the whole universe will be filled with Christ. God created all things so that all things will express Christ. God created man in order that man would be like His Son, having the life of His Son and the glory of His Son, so that the only begotten Son can become the firstborn Son among many sons. God created man and redeemed him for Christ. Redemption is for the purpose of reaching the goal of creation. Christ is the Bridegroom, and we are the friends of the Groom. He is the chief cornerstone, and each one of us is one of the millions of stones. God created us for the satisfaction of Christ's heart. We are thankful that we have seen the relationship between Christ and us. We praise Him because we have seen the relationship between God and Christ. God's center is Christ. God's goal is centered upon Christ. God's goal has two aspects: (1) that all things would express the glory of Christ and (2) that man would be like Christ, having the life of Christ and the glory of Christ. ❧

(Morning, January 24)

Scripture Reading:

The First Group: *Concerning God's Plan: Ephesians 3:9-11 ("purpose" can be translated as "plan"); 1:8-11 ("will" can be translated as "plan"); Revelation 4:11 ("will" can be translated as "pleasure"); 1 Corinthians 8:6; Romans 11:36*

The Second Group: *Concerning God's Plan to Hand Over All Things to Christ: Ephesians 4:10; John 3:35; 13:3; 16:15; 17:7; Hebrews 1:2*

The Third Group: *Concerning Christ Creating All Things: Hebrews 1:2b, 3b; John 1:1-3, 10; Colossians 1:16-17; 1 Corinthians 8:6b*

The Fourth Group: *Concerning Christ Creating Man: 1 Corinthians 11:3; Galatians 4:4-7; Romans 8:28b-30 ("purpose" can be translated as "plan"); 1 Peter 1:2a; 1 Corinthians 1:9; Hebrews 2:5-10; 1 Corinthians 3:21-23*

The Fifth Group: *Concerning the Condition in Eternity after Redemption: Philippians 2:9-11; Revelation 4:11; 5:12-14; 1 John 3:2*

The Sixth Group: *Concerning God's Ordination before the Foundation of the World: John 17:24; Ephesians 1:4-5; Titus 1:2; 2 Timothy 1:9-10; 1 Peter 1:20*

The Seventh Group: *Concerning God's Ordination since the Foundation of the World: Matthew 25:34; Hebrews 4:3; 9:26; Revelation 13:8; 17:8*

CHRIST BEFORE THE FOUNDATION OF THE WORLD

Christ Having the First Place in God's Plan

Before the foundation of the world, God had a plan. This plan was to head up all things in heaven and on earth, under Christ and in Christ. This plan is based on His pleasure. God is the First Cause; everything is of Him and out of Him. This is the meaning of the first group of verses.

In eternity past, God ordained that there be a house and that the second person of the Godhead, the Son, rule over this house. God committed all things to the Son, and the Son inherits all things. Everything is of the Son, through the Son, and unto the Son. The Father plans, the Son inherits what the Father planned, and the Spirit accomplishes what the Father planned. The Father is the planning One, the Son is the inheriting One, and the Spirit is the accomplishing One. From eternity past, the Father has loved the Son; He is the "Beloved of the Father." God has loved Him from eternity past. When the Son came to earth, the Father still declared, "My Son, the Beloved" (Matt. 3:17). The Father loves the Son and has given Him all things. Before the Lord died, He knew "that the Father had given all into His hands" (John 13:3). When He resurrected and ascended, it was so that "He might fill all things" (Eph. 4:10). This is the meaning of the second group of verses.

CHRIST IN CREATION

Christ Having the First Place in All Things and in the Creation of Man

After the Father made a plan, the Son came to create. The Father planned creation according to His own will. The Son agreed with this and created, while the Spirit's power accomplished it. The Son is the One who created all things. In creation the Son is the Firstborn of all creation (Col. 1:15), and the beginning of the creation of God (Rev. 3:14). According to His eternal plan and before the foundation of the world, God ordained that the Son become flesh and accomplish redemption (1 Pet. 1:20). In God's plan the Son was the first in creation. Therefore, He is the Head of all creation. God planned, and the Son created. Creation was completed for the Son. God created all things in order to satisfy the Son's heart. Oh! the Lord is so great! He is the Alpha and the Omega! He is the Alpha because all things are of Him. He is the Omega because all things are unto Him. This is the meaning of the third group of verses.

God created man in order that man would be like Christ, having His life and His glory. God expresses Himself through Christ, while Christ expresses Himself through man. God called us to partake of His Son that we would become like His Son and that His Son would be the Firstborn among many brothers. From eternity past until the resurrection, the Lord was the only Begotten. When the Lord was resurrected from the dead, He became the Firstborn. This is why after His resurrection, He said, "Go to My *brothers* and say to them, I ascend to My Father and your Father, and My God and your God" (John 20:17). The many sons became sons in the only begotten Son. God caused the only begotten Son to die in order that many sons could be produced. God has made us not only the sons but the heirs as well. God has not only given us the life of the Son but has also caused us to inherit the inheritance with the Son. The Son was made a man, a little lower than the angels for a while. After that He received honor and glory as His crown and will lead many sons into glory. The reason God created man was that man would have the life of His Son and enter into glory with His Son, thus satisfying His Son's heart. Thank God that He created and redeemed us for the satisfaction of Christ's heart. ❀

(Morning, January 25)

God predestinated man to be conformed to the image of His Son. (God's predestination is according to His foreknowledge. His predestination concerns our destiny. His selection concerns us as men. His predestination concerns us in eternity. His calling concerns us in this age.) God wants us to be conformed to the image of His Son, which means that He uses His Son as the mold. From this mold He reproduces us as the many sons, making his Son the Firstborn among many sons. God wants us not only to have His Son's life, but His Son's glory as well (Rom. 8:29-30). God wants His Son to lead many sons into glory. God's Son is "He who sanctifies," and we are "those who are being sanctified." Both are of One, and both are from the same Father. Therefore, He is not ashamed to call us brothers (Heb. 2:11). Christ in us is making us the sons of God. In the future He will lead us into glory. Therefore, Christ in us becomes the hope of glory (Col. 1:27). Today we are God's sons; one day we will be glorified with Christ (Rom. 8:16-17). God wants to dispense His Son's life to many people, making them God's many sons so that His Son may become the Firstborn among many sons, having the first place in all things.

The individual Christ is different from the corporate Christ. First Corinthians 12:12 speaks of the corporate Christ who is composed of the individual Christ and the church. *The Christ* here means the church. When we were born, we were all Adam. Today because of Christ's life in us, we are all Christ. Adam was the first man; Christ is the second Man and also the last Man (1 Cor. 15:47, 45). Before Christ's death and resurrection, there was only one individual Christ. After His death and resurrection, He imparted His life to many and became the corporate Christ. The above plus yesterday's closing words are the meaning of the fourth group of verses.

God's plan originated *before* the foundation of the world. At that time God loved the Son (John 17:24) and predestinated Him to be Christ (1 Pet. 1:19-20). God then chose us unto sonship (Eph. 1:4-5). (Selection is to select us as men, while predestination is to call us unto sonship.) In eternity past God gave us grace (2 Tim. 1:9-11) and predestinated us to share in His life, not in His Person (Titus 1:2). God foreknew that Satan would rebel, breaking the harmony between God and all things. God foreknew that man would fall and become sinful. Consequently, before the foundation of the world, God conferred with His Son and sent Him to the cross to reconcile all things to His Son, redeem fallen man, and deal with the rebellious Satan. This is the meaning of the sixth group of verses.

God accomplished His plan *since* the foundation of the world. The Lord was slain from the foundation of the world (Rev. 13:8). Our names have been written in the book of life from the foundation of the world (Rev. 13:8). (Our selection was made *before* the foundation of the world.) God's works of creation were completed from the foundation of the world (Heb. 4:3). His eternal kingdom has been prepared from the foundation of the world (Matt. 25:34). This is the meaning of the seventh group of verses.

CHRIST IN ETERNITY

Christ Having the First Place in Eternity

After the Lord's death and resurrection, "God highly exalted Him and bestowed on Him the name which is above every name, that in the name of Jesus every knee should bow, of those who are in heaven and on earth and under the earth, and every tongue should openly confess that Jesus Christ is Lord to the glory of God the Father" (Phil. 2:9-11). God has made Him both Lord and Christ (Acts 2:36) and has put all things under His feet (Eph. 1:20-22). Revelation 4 and 5 show the scene of the Lord's ascension into the heavens after His resurrection, in which He receives glory and praise. Chapter four shows the praise of all the creatures for creation. Chapter five reveals their praises for redemption. God wants to put the enemy underneath the Lord's feet (Matt. 22:44). Concerning this matter, the church today bears a great responsibility. God is waiting for the church to fulfill this work.

Since Satan's rebellion and the fall of man, all things have been subjected to vanity. This means that their former goal has been lost and that they have no definite direction. Today all things are subject to vanity and are waiting for God's sons to be manifested. In this waiting period, all creation is under the slavery of corruption. We see this in the decreasing intensity of sunlight and in the withering of plant life. However, all things have a hope that one day they will be freed from the slavery of corruption. While having this hope, all things groan and travail in pain. When God's children enter the freedom of the glory, all things will be freed. In the day of the redemption of our bodies, all creation will be set free. But today we can have a foretaste of the power of the coming age. (The church is a foretaste of the power of the coming age, while the kingdom is a foretaste of the power of eternity.) One day our bodies will be redeemed; we will receive full sonship and will enter into the freedom of the glory (Rom. 8:19-23).

When the Lord appears we shall be like Him (1 John 3:2). On the one hand, we are His sons and have His life and nature. On the other hand, we are His heirs, inheriting God's inheritance in glory (1 Pet. 1:3-4).

Revelation 21 and 22 show us a picture of eternity, not of the millennium. These two chapters speak of four crucial points: (1) God; (2) the Lamb; (3) the city, the physical city with its citizens, the ones God had predestinated before the foundation of the world and whom He gained; these are also the thirsty ones mentioned in Revelation 7; and (4) the nations. God and the Lamb are the center of the city. Revelation 21:9-22 speaks about the city. Verse 23 speaks about the center of the city. God's glory is the light, and the Lamb is the lamp. Light comes through the lamp, signifying God being revealed through the Lamb. The center of the new creation is the New Jerusalem which is composed of God's sons. The center of this city is God and the Lamb. The glorious light of God is in the Lamb. The Lamb lights the city, and the bright city shines on the nations. In the city there is only one street and one river. There is only one street, so no man will become lost. This street must be shaped like a spiral. The river is in the middle of the street and flows along with the street. Both the street and the river proceed out of the throne of God and of the Lamb. Thus God and the Lamb are the center.

After all things have been subjected to the Lord, He Himself will willingly be subjected to God (1 Cor. 15:28). This is the meaning of the fifth group of verses.

Therefore, we see that from eternity to eternity, all the things God has done are for His Son to have the first place in all things. God's goal is to make His Son the King over all things. ❦

(Morning, January 26)

CHRIST IN REDEMPTION

Christ Having the First Place in Redemption

A few days ago we saw that "Christ is all and in all." What God planned before the foundation of the world is "that He Himself might have the first place in all things." Today we want to see how Christ's redemption accomplishes God's plan.

God's plan has one goal with two aspects: (1) to have all things expressing Christ's glory, so that Christ may have the first place in all things, and (2) to have man conformed to Christ, having His life and His glory.

Colossians 1 tells us these two things: (1) Christ has the first place in all things, and (2) Christ is the Head of the church.

Ephesians 1 also tells us these two things: (1) Christ is heading up all things in the heavens and on earth, and (2) the church becomes His inheritance.

Revelation 4 and 5 also tell us these two things: (1) chapter four speaks of creation, and (2) chapter five speaks of redemption.

God's creation is for the carrying out of His plan. God's goal in creating all things and man, is to have all things express Christ and to have man conformed to Christ, having His life and glory. However, Satan rebelled and came in to interrupt, causing all things to become disjointed and causing man to fall. Therefore, God had to use redemption to achieve the goal of His creation. As a result, Christ's redemption must (1) reconcile all things to God, and (2) redeem fallen mankind and impart His life to them. To solve God's problems, Christ's redemption must also (3) deal with the rebellious Satan, and (4) take care of man's sin.

Christ's redemption indeed solved these four matters. It accomplished God's goals: (1) by reconciling all things to God, and (2) by dispensing His life to man. It also solved God's problems: (3) by dealing with the rebellious Satan, and (4) by taking care of man's sin. Two are positive and two are negative.

Christ's Redemption Accomplishing God's Two Goals

Before the foundation of the world, the Father had a conference with His Son, in which He asked His Son to come as a man to accomplish redemption. Redemption is not a temporary remedy that God made in time, but a plan according to His predestination. Christ did not come to the world to become a man according to Adam's image; rather, Adam was created according to Christ's image. Genesis 1:26 is God's plan, while 1:27 is God's execution of His plan. Verse 26 says that it is "Us" that plan, while verse 27 says God created according to "His" image. Verse 26 tells of the plan in the conference of the Godhead, while verse 27 tells of the creation of man according to the Son's image. Within the Godhead, only the Son has an image. Adam was created according to Christ's image. That is why Adam is a type of Christ (Rom. 5:14). Christ's coming to the world was not a temporary remedy; it was out of God's plan. Christ was anointed before the foundation of the world. He is the universal Man. He is not limited by time and space. He is the anointed One from before the foundation of the world. He is also the Christ who fills the universe. Bethlehem and Judea are both universal. Not only was Christ born in Bethlehem and baptized in the Jordan River; the universe was also born and baptized there. The Christ in the Gospels should be considered as the universal Christ.

The first thing in Christ's redemption is His incarnation. Christ was incarnated to be a man in order to come from the position of the Creator to the position of the creature. He had to take on a created body before He could die for man and for all things. There must first be Bethlehem before there can be Golgotha. There must first be the manger before there can be the cross.

(1) Christ's redemption reconciled all things to God. All things were created in Christ (Col. 1:16). When God deals with Christ, He deals with all things. All things are dealt with by God in Christ, just as Levi had offered up tithes in Abraham's loins (Heb. 7:9-10). Christ tasted death on behalf of everything (Heb. 2:9). On the cross He reconciled all things to God (Col. 1:20). The extent of Christ's redemption covers not only man but all things as well. All things have not sinned; therefore, redemption is not needed for them. The problem between all things and God is that they are not reconciled. Therefore, they need only reconciliation.

(2) Christ's redemption gives man His life. Christ's redemption not only reconciles all things to God, but also causes man to have life and to be like Him. Redemption releases His life. When Christ was on the earth, His divine life was restricted and confined

to His flesh. When He was in Jerusalem, He could not be in Galilee. Christ's death enabled this confined life to be released.

"The grain of wheat" in John 12:24 is God's only begotten Son. The life of this grain of wheat is confined to its shell. If it does not fall into the ground and die, it will forever be one grain. If it dies, and its flesh is broken, the life within will be released, thus producing many grains. All these grains will be identical to that one grain. We can also say that every grain is in that one grain. Christ died to reproduce us. Before His death He was the only begotten Son. After His resurrection He became the Firstborn among many sons. Christ's resurrection regenerates us so that we can obtain His life.

"Fire" in Luke 12:49 refers to Christ's life. When Christ was on earth, His life was confined to His outer shell. Through His baptism—His death on the cross—this confined life was released. Christ's life was released and was cast on the earth. After being cast on the earth, it was kindled. This caused division on the earth. Christ's death is a great release of His life! As a result of His death, His life was imparted to us.

Christ's Redemption Solving God's Two Problems

The above shows Christ's redemption accomplishing God's two goals. Let us go on to see how Christ's redemption solves God's two problems.

(1) Christ's redemption has dealt with the rebellious Satan. What overcomes Satan is not the cross but the blood. Satan knew that if his poison were injected into the first couple, this poison would spread to all their descendants. Satan committed spiritual fornication with our forefather and put this sinful poison of lying into his soul. The life of the soul is in the blood. Man's life is passed on through the blood (Acts 17:26). Consequently, the sinful poison of this first couple has passed on to us through the blood.

Christ's blood has no poison; it is precious and incorruptible. He bore the sins of many on the cross and died, emptying all of His blood. When He resurrected from the dead, He was without blood. After His resurrection He had bones and flesh, but no blood. "He poured out His soul unto death" (Isa. 53:12). In Christ, our blood has been poured out. Satan has no ground to work in us. Christ's blood has destroyed and dealt with Satan and all he has.

(2) Christ's redemption has dealt with man's sins. Our sins need Christ's death. The substitutionary death of Christ abolished all the records of our sins before God. The representative death of Christ, the Head, has delivered us from our sins.

Christ's death accomplishes God's two goals and solves God's two problems. This is Christ's victory. This victory has already been accomplished. God keeps us on the earth to maintain this victory and to preach it to every creature (Col. 1:23). Our baptism and the breaking of bread are to display the victory of Christ's death to the angels, the devil, the nations, and all things.

The Goals of Redemption

The goals of Christ's redemption are that we be His particular people (Titus 2:14) and living sacrifice (Rom. 12:1), that we would live to Him and die to Him (Rom. 14:7-9), that we would be the temple of the Holy Spirit glorifying God (1 Cor. 6:19-20), that we would live to Him (2 Cor. 5:15), and that whether through life or through death, Christ would be magnified in our body, so that for us to live is Christ (Phil. 1:20-21).

The goal of redemption is to give Christ the first place in all things. In order that Christ may have the first place in all things, He must first have the preeminence in us. We are the firstfruit among all things. First we must be subjected to Christ, then all things can be subjected to Christ. The cross enables God to reach this goal in us. The cross makes us decrease and makes Christ increase. The cross will find room for Christ and will ensure that Christ has the first place. God works through the cross, which in turn works through the environment to dig into us deeply, causing us to know Christ and be filled with Him, so that Christ may have the first place in us. Christ's redemption has accomplished God's plan before the foundation of the world. This plan is to give Him the first place in all things. We should forget about our personal interests and care only for the accomplishment of God's eternal destiny which is to have Christ gain the first place in all things. When we see the Messiah, we will cast away our waterpot! When we see God's Christ, we will cast away everything! ❦

(Morning, January 27)

CHRIST IN THE CHRISTIAN LIFE AND EXPERIENCE

Christ Having the First Place in the Life and Experience of the Christians

Christ Having the First Place in the Christian Life

Scripture Reading:
2 Corinthians 5:14-15; Galatians 2:20

The life of a Christian is Christ (Col. 3:4). Christ being our life and Christ being our power are two different things. How can we be holy? How can we be victorious?

(1) Many think that holiness and victory mean being delivered from the little sins and dealing with the temper.

(2) Some think that holiness and victory mean being patient, humble, and meek.

(3) Some think that holiness and victory mean putting the self and the flesh to death.

(4) Some think that holiness and victory mean studying the Bible more, praying more, being careful, and trusting in the Lord for one's strength.

(5) Some know that power is with the Lord, that our flesh has

been crucified on the cross, and that by faith, we should claim the Lord's power to overcome and be holy.

None of the above five cases is right. The fifth case may seem to be right, but actually it is not for the following reason:

Christ is our life. This is victory! This is holiness! The victorious life, the holy life, the perfect life, are all Christ. From beginning to end, everything is Christ. Outside of Christ, we have nothing. Christ must have the first place in all things. The victorious life God has given us is not a thing, such as patience or meekness, but the living Christ. Christ never mends our wrongs. What we lack is not patience but a living Christ. God will never tear a piece of cloth from Christ to mend our hole. To be short of patience is to be short of Christ, because God wants Christ to have the first place in all things. Therefore, to put the self to death is not holiness. Holiness is Christ. Christ must have the first place in all things.

If God were to cause us to have power, it would only make us powerful persons; Christ would not have the first place in us. Christ is my power; it is Christ who holds the first place in me. We do not have power because we are not weak enough. The power of Christ "is made perfect in weakness." It is not that the Lord *makes* me powerful; but it is the Lord who is the power in my stead.

Mr. Hudson Taylor saw that "You *are* the branches." The author of *The Victorious Life* saw that victory is just Christ. It is not that I draw power from Christ to help me be a man; rather, it is Christ who is the man *in my place.* It is not that Christ gives me the power to be patient; rather, it is Christ who lives the patience out from me. "Lord, I allow You to live out from me!" We do not overcome by the Lord; rather, it is the Lord who overcomes through us! It is not us overcoming through Him; rather, it is Him overcoming through us. By faith I commit myself to the Lord and allow the Lord to live Himself out of me. I do not live by Christ; rather, "it is Christ who lives in me" (Gal. 2:20). I live because of the life of Christ and also because of "the faith in the Son of God" (v. 20b). When we believed and received the Son of God, not only did His life enter into us, but His faith also entered into us. Therefore, we can live because of His faith.

Victory is Christ! Patience is Christ! What we need is not patience, meekness, or love, but Christ. Christ must have the first place in all things. From within us, Christ lives out patience, meekness, and love. Man deserves only to die. There is nothing else that he deserves. After God created Adam, He had a will, and Adam had to obey this will. But when God re-created us, it was not like this. He put us in death, and God Himself lives out His will from within us. We should not only see a substitutionary Savior on Mount Golgotha, we should also see a Lord within us who lives in our stead. Christ is our wisdom. In the past He was our righteousness for our salvation. In the present He is our sanctification for us to live a holy life. In the future He will be our redemption that our body may be redeemed (1 Cor. 1:30). He holds the first place in all things!

How can we enter into this victorious life? We must do the following things:

1. Have Absolutely No Hope in Our Self

We must know the self thoroughly. We must see that the self deserves only to die; any hope in the self must come to an end. Our end is God's beginning. We cannot receive the victory of Christ if we still have hope in our self. Christ is living in us, but we have not given Him the ground to rule over us and reign within us.

2. Have a Full Consecration

We must consecrate wholeheartedly. If we do not see our utter weakness, we cannot accept the cross and fully consecrate ourselves, nor hand over all our rights to the Lord's hand to allow Him to be the Lord.

3. Believe

After consecration we have to believe that Christ is being lived out in us and that He has taken over our rights.

Christ is to be lived out in our flesh in the same way that He was lived out of the flesh given Him through Mary. Christ today wants to live Himself out on the earth through our flesh as He did in His own flesh while on earth. Christ has to be lived out in our lives. Our victory is based on our yielding to Christ the first place in all things and allowing Him to be the Lord in all of our living.

The Old Testament tells us how God's chosen people lived on the earth. There was first the tabernacle as the center of the twelve tribes. Later the temple was their center. The center of the temple was the ark. The tabernacle, the temple, and the ark all typify Christ. When the relationship between the Israelites and the tabernacle or the temple was proper, they were victorious; no nation could overcome them. Although their enemies had learned warfare and they had not, they still overcame all their enemies. When something was wrong between them and the temple, they were carried away. It did not depend on whether or not they had a competent king; neither did it depend on whether or not they were clever and able. It depended only on whether or not something was wrong between them and the ark in the temple. We must allow the Lord to have the first place. Only then will we be victorious. We must be concerned about the Lord's victory before we can have the victory. Once the hair of separation is shaven, there can be no victory. The same is true with us today. If we do not give Christ the highest place, we cannot be victorious. If Christ does not have the first place in our heart, we cannot be victorious.

(Morning, January 29)

Christ Having the First Place in the Christian Experience

Scripture Reading: John 3:30

The experience of a Christian has two sides: one is sweet, the other, painful. God causes us to experience a sweet and suffering life in order that Christ may have the first place in all things.

The Experience on the Sweet Side

Answers to Prayers

The goal of prayer to let Christ have the first place in all things must be reached, before it will be answered. Seek first God's kingdom and God's righteousness, then God will add to us all that we need. (To add is not to give but to add to something that is already there; while to give is to give something that is not there.) To ask in the Lord's name is to ask the Father on behalf of the Lord that the Lord may gain something. According to this principle, those who care for the flesh have nothing to pray. They must let the cross cut away the flesh before they can become the Lord's intercessors, praying in His will rather than praying for their own purpose. Only those who let Christ have the first place in all things can enter into the Holy of Holies. We should turn the time we pray for our own need into the time we pray for God's business. God will listen both to the prayers that we utter (the prayers we pray that are for God's business) as well as the prayers that we do not utter (the prayers we pray that are for our own affairs). We should let the Lord gain something first. Afterward, the Lord will let us gain something. The sweetest part of the Christian life is to receive answers to prayer continually. But God's purpose in answering our prayers is that Christ may have the first place in all things.

Growth

Growth is also a sweet side of the Christian life. We should be like children but not be childish. Growth is not having biblical knowledge but having more of Christ, to be filled with Christ. Growth is less of self, even none of self. It is to think less of self, even to think nothing of the self. Humility is to not look at the self. To see oneself is to be relatively humble; not to see oneself is to be absolutely humble. To grow is to let Christ have the first place in us. "He must increase, but I must decrease" (John 3:30). It is not how much biblical knowledge we have, but how much consecration we have, how much we have put in God's hand, and how much we have allowed Christ to have the first place. The real growth is to let Christ be magnified.

Receiving Light

There is also the receiving of light from God—spiritual vision—which is another sweet side of the Christian life. Revelation is something given to us by God objectively. Light is the revelation God shows to us subjectively. Vision is what we see when we are enlightened by God's light; it includes light and revelation. First there is the enlightening, then the faith. To be continually under the enlightening we must allow Christ to have the first place in all things continually. "If therefore your eye is single, your whole body will be full of light" (Matt. 6:22). It is not that we do not understand, but that we cannot understand, because the eye is not single. "The pure in heart...shall see God" (Matt. 5:8). The heart must be pure. "If anyone resolves to do His will, he will know" (John 7:17). Only those who let Christ have the first place can have light.

Having Power

Power is also a sweet side of the Christian life. In order to have power, we must let Christ be enthroned. When He increases, we have the power. Without separation, there can be no power. To be separated is not only to come out, but to come in—to be in Christ. We are different from others because we are in Christ and have put on Christ. Christ is our power.

The Experience on the Suffering Side

Material Sufferings

In general all believers have financial difficulties. Perhaps this is because the things they formerly did were improper, things they now can no longer do. Or perhaps it is because of spiritual reasons, where God is behind the scene directing matters with some specific goal. God takes away our material possessions so that we will seek

Christ that He may have the first place in all things. It is not impossible for a rich man to enter the kingdom of God, but it is difficult. It is not impossible for him to serve the Lord, but it is difficult. Cast your treasure in the dust, and Jehovah will be your treasure (Job 22:24-25). In the wilderness God dealt with the children of Israel by stripping them of all the earthly supply of food and clothing in order that they might know God's riches. When the earthly supply stops, the heavenly supply comes. Difficulty in material supplies comes for the purpose that we may seek to have Christ take the first place in all things and learn the lessons of faith. When difficulty comes, we should believe that it is from God and rejoice. But we should not hope for difficulties to come. If we do, Satan also can cause difficulties to be added to us.

Emotional Sufferings

The reason we lose our parents, husband, wife, children, and relatives is that God wants us to take Christ as our satisfaction. God takes these away from us in order that we would take Christ as Lord and allow Him to have the first place in us. God has no intention to deal with us severely; His intention is only for us to take Christ as Lord. To weep before the Lord is more precious than to be happy before men. What we find in the Lord is what cannot be found in our parents, wife, and children. Both in creation and in His dealing with the believers, God wants His Son to have the first place. If we offer up Isaac, we will receive back Isaac. God does not let us have anything outside of His Son.

Physical Sufferings

God allows sickness and weakness to come to our body in order that we may learn to (1) pray at night, (2) be watchful as sparrows on the rooftop, (3) know that the Lord makes our bed for us, (4) deal with sin, (5) wait quietly, (6) touch the hem of the Lord's garment, (7) know that the Lord sent His word to heal us, (8) know that through sickness God causes us to become useful persons, (9) know that holiness is healing, and (10) know that the Lord's resurrection power removes our weakness, sickness, and death. Through sicknesses, God causes us to learn to trust, rely, and obey, so that Christ may have the first place in us.

Suffering through the Loss of Natural Goodness

After a person is saved, he always exercises his natural virtues. But after some time, perhaps a few years, the Lord will remove his natural virtues. This will make him suffer. The Lord deprives us of our virtues in Adam that we may see our own corruption. God takes away our goodness that we may be filled with Christ.

God deprives us of our possessions, relatives, health, and goodness in order that we would take Christ as our satisfaction, be filled with Christ, and allow Him to have the first place in all things.

Whatever God gives to us, whether it be a sweet life or a suffering life, is for the purpose of making Christ the One who occupies the first place in us. ❋

(Morning, January 30)

CHRIST IN CHRISTIAN WORK AND MESSAGES

Christ Having the First Place in Christian Work and Messages

Scripture Reading:
Ephesians 2:10; 1 Corinthians 2:2; 2 Corinthians 4:5

Life and experience are inward matters, while the work and messages are outward matters. Whether it be inward matters or outward matters, we should allow Christ to have the first place in all things.

Christ Having the First Place in Christian Work

Christ should have the first place in our work. "Good works,...that we would walk in them" (Eph. 2:10). "Good works" are just Christ. The goal of God's work is Christ, and we should walk in this work. All believers, no matter what profession they hold, are doing the work of God and should walk in God's good works. To serve God and to work for God are two vastly different matters. Many work for God but do not serve God. Whether or not a work is of faithfulness depends upon the intent, motive, and purpose and if the goal is for Christ. In doing God's work, although there is suffering, there is also joy; although there is difficulty, there is also comfort. There is also the attraction to God's work. We often work because of our interest, not because of Christ. Many times men run to and fro to work for a name for themselves. They have worked, but they have not served God. God's work from eternity to eternity has always been with the view that His Son would have the first place in all things. Therefore, our work should also be for Christ. If God does not purify our intent and motive, we cannot receive God's blessing. We work not for sinners but for Christ. How successful our work is depends on how much Christ is in it. We should allow the Holy Spirit to discern our intention right from the beginning, to see if it belongs to the spirit or to the soul, and to see if it belongs to this side or to that side. Our work should not be for our own increase, our own group, or our own message; rather, we should work for Christ. As long as God gains something, we should rejoice. When we see God gaining something, even if it is not through our hands, we should be happy for it. We are not saving our message but saving sinners; we are not here to gain our own heart but Christ's heart. When things go our way and we gain something, it means that the Lord gains nothing and nothing goes His way. If we would take God's gain as our satisfaction, we would not be proud or jealous. Many times we seek God's glory as well as our own glory. God saves men for Christ, not for us. Paul planted, and Apollos watered. It was not accomplished by one person, lest anyone would say, "I am of Paul," or "I am of Apollos." All the things concerning the work are for Christ, not for the worker. We are the loaves in the Lord's hand. When people eat the loaves, they thank the one who gives them the loaves; they do not thank the loaves, which are we. The work from its beginning to its end is all for Christ, not for us. We should be satisfied with the work allotted to us by the Lord and with the position the Lord arranged for us. We should not be "in another man's rule" (2 Cor. 10:16). We like very much to leave our own lot to tread on another's lot. The question is not whether we can do it or know how to do it, but whether God has commanded it. Sisters should stand in the sisters' position (1 Cor. 14:34-35). Sisters should not be teachers, making judgments concerning God's word (1 Tim. 2:12). In all the work, we should let Christ have the first place.

Christ Having the First Place in Christian Messages

Christ should also have the first place in our messages. We "preach...Christ Jesus as Lord" (2 Cor. 4:5). "For I did not determine to know anything among you except Jesus Christ, and this One crucified" (1 Cor. 2:2). Christ is the center of God's plan and the center of God's goal. The cross is the center of God's work. The work of the cross is to accomplish God's goal. The cross works to eliminate all that issues from the flesh in order that Christ may have the first place. Our central message should not be the dispensations, the prophecies, the types, the kingdom, baptism, forsaking denominations, speaking in tongues, keeping the Sabbath, or holiness, etc. Our central message should be Christ. The centrality of God is Christ. Therefore, we should take Him as the center.

After a person is saved, we should help him to consecrate himself to be a slave of Christ, so that he receives Christ as his Lord in all things.

All the truths in the Bible are related like a wheel with spokes and a hub, having Christ as the center. We are not neglecting the truths outside the center; rather, we need to link these truths with the center. Concerning any truth we should know two things: (1) we should know about this truth, and (2) we should know how this truth relates to the center. We should pay attention to the center. Of course, this does not mean we do not speak of other truths. Paul said, "I did not determine to know anything among you except Jesus Christ, and this One crucified" (1 Cor. 2:2). Later he also said, "But we do speak wisdom among those who are full-grown" (2:6). It is only after a person has consecrated himself and received Christ as his Lord that we can speak to him the truths concerning his building up. In our work we should continually draw people back to the center and let them see that "Christ is Lord." We cannot do this work in an objective way. We ourselves must be the first to be broken by God and allow Christ to have the first place in us, before we can lead others to receive Christ as Lord and allow Christ to have the first place in them. We must live out a life of giving Christ the first place before we can spread this message. Our message is just our person. We should allow Christ to have the first place in the small things in our daily life before we can preach the message of the centrality of Christ. I only wish that every one of us would give the Lord Jesus His place on the throne! If the will of God is to be accomplished, what does it matter if I am put in the dust? The Lord's "well done" surpasses all the praises of the world. The smiling face of heaven surpasses all the angry faces of the earth. The comfort of heaven surpasses the tears of the earth. The hidden manna is enjoyed in eternity. May the Lord bless His word that He would gain us and others also. ❧

(Morning, January 31)

3

THE OVERCOMER OF GOD

"...the church, which is His Body,
the fullness of the One who fills all in all."
Ephesians 1:23

GOD'S ETERNAL PLAN AND THE CHURCH

Scripture Reading:
Ephesians 1:23

God's Eternal Plan

God had an eternal plan before the foundation of the world. There are two goals in this plan. The first is to make all things express Christ, and the second is to make man like Christ, that man would have His life and glory. While God desires to accomplish these two goals, He encounters two problems: Satan's rebellion and man's fall.

On the day the archangel saw that Christ was the center of all things, he became jealous because of his pride. He wanted to raise himself to the same position as God's Son. He rebelled because he wanted to rob Christ of His position as the center. One-third of the angels followed him to rebel against God, and on that day all the living creatures on the earth also followed him. Satan's rebellion made everything a chaos, which could not express Christ. The universe is one big entity. We learn from science that if one speck of dust is out of order, the whole universe can become chaotic and be in confusion. Today, even though all things can express God's glory, they cannot express God Himself.

God created man in order that first he would have the life and glory of Christ, and He intended to put all things under man's subjection so that man would bring everything back to God. Second, He created man so that man would cooperate with God to deal with the rebellious Satan.

But man also fell. Therefore, now God has to accomplish two goals and solve two problems. In order to accomplish His two goals, God has to (1) save fallen man and (2) remove the rebellious Satan.

In order to carry out God's two goals and solve His two problems, the Lord Jesus became a man and accomplished redemption. The Lord Jesus is not only the Christ to mankind, but also the Christ to all things. Christ is the centrality and the universality. Universality means that He is not limited by time or space. Christ is not only the Christ of the Jews or the Christ of the church, but He is also the Christ of all things. He is all and in all.

There are three aspects to Christ's redemption: (1) substitution, for the individual; (2) representation, for the church; and (3) heading up, for all things. Christ as the Head includes all things. When the Head died, everything included in the Head died also. Christ's death is an all-inclusive death. Christ's death as the Head brought all things and mankind into death, so that all things and mankind are now reconciled to God.

Christ dealt with everything on the cross. He crushed the serpent's head and dealt with the rebellious Satan and all his works on the cross. He saved fallen mankind on the cross. He brought back all things and reconciled them to God on the cross. On the cross He gave His life to man so that man can be like Him.

Therefore, we can see that God has two goals and also two problems. By means of the cross, Christ accomplished God's two goals and also solved God's two problems.

The Church's Position and Responsibility

In what position has God put the church? What mission does God want the church to bear on the earth? Why did God allow Satan, whose head had been crushed, to remain on the earth?

God wants the church on earth not only to preach the gospel to save sinners but also to testify of Christ's victory on the cross. God allows Satan to remain on the earth in order to provide us the opportunities to testify to His Son's victory. God expects that we would testify to His Son's victory. All failing believers damage this testimony.

The church is the Body of Christ. The Body should continue the work of the Head. The church is the fullness of Christ. What overflows from Christ is the church. The church should continue the works of the four Gospels.

There are three very crucial things in the New Testament: (1) the cross, (2) the church, and (3) the kingdom. Christ on the cross accomplished redemption and victory. The kingdom is for the manifestation of the accomplishment of Christ's redemption and His victory. At present, the church is maintaining on earth Christ's accomplishment on the cross. The cross is God's proper judgment according to the law, while the kingdom is the execution of God's authority. The church lies in the middle; it maintains the accomplishment of the cross on the one hand and is a foretaste of the power of the coming age on the other hand.

Satan cannot overcome the individual Christ, but he can insult the individual Christ through the corporate Christ. Failure of the Body is failure to the Head. A member's failure is the Body's failure. We are the continuation of Christ. We are to extend Christ (Isa. 53:10) just as we extended Adam. God allows us to remain on earth for the purpose of accomplishing His eternal plan and achieving His eternal goal.

Before the ark entered Jerusalem, it was in the house of Obed-edom the Gittite (2 Sam. 6). We should be faithful to take care of the blood upon the ark (Christ's work) and the cherubim upon the ark (God's glory). ❋

(Afternoon, January 24)

THE NATURE OF CHRIST'S VICTORY AND THE CHURCH

Scripture Reading: Revelation 3:21

All victories should take the victory of Christ as a pattern: "As I also overcame."

Three Enemies

The Bible tells us that we have three different enemies: (1) the flesh, within us, (2) the world, outside of us, and (3) Satan, above and below us. As far as the church's ascended position is concerned, Satan is below us.

There were three nations in the Old Testament that typified these three enemies. Amalek typifies the flesh; we should overcome it with our prayer. Egypt typifies the world; it should be buried in the Red Sea. The Canaanites typify the powers of Satan; they should be overcome and removed one by one.

The flesh is against the Spirit (Gal. 5:17). The world is against the Father. If any man loves the world, the love for the Father is not in him (1 John 2:15). Satan is against Christ. Christ came to destroy Satan (1 John 3:8). Therefore, subjection to the Spirit is victory over the flesh, the love for the Father is victory over the world, and faith in Christ is victory over Satan.

The first thing that came in was the flesh. One day, the archangel tried to uplift himself to be like God by means of the "self," and the "self" entered the world. This was the beginning of sin, the world, and Satan.

At the time God created man, He bestowed on him the highest ability, the ability to reproduce, by which he can pass his life on to his offspring. Originally God expected man to eat the fruit of the tree of life so that he would have God's life to pass on to his offspring. God forbade him to eat the tree of the knowledge of good and evil. But Satan came and committed spiritual fornication with the first couple in their soul. Satan put his poisonous seed within them so that they passed this on to their offspring. Satan is the father of liars. The seed of Satan is lies. The seed of God is truth. The principle with which Satan beguiled Adam to sin is the same principle as that which caused Satan himself to sin at the beginning.

Satan has his household and kingdom. He gains men to be the members of his household and citizens of his kingdom so that he can be the king over them.

After Satan beguiled man to sin, his work was confined from the universe to just the earth, the world. He was cursed: "Upon your stomach you will go, / And dust you will eat / All the days of your life" (Gen. 3:14). He could only move on the earth and could only have man, who comes out of the dust, for his food. This was a great defeat for Satan. Man's fall is a great victory for God.

Satan has his system on the earth. His organization becomes the present world. Satan is the king of this organization, while the whole world lies under his hand.

The Victory of Christ

Before the Lord Jesus began to minister, He was baptized. This means that His work during the three and a half years was carried out after His death and resurrection. As a result, there was no flesh in His work. We can call this three and a half years as a living of the cross. The Lord Jesus never walked according to His will but according to the will of Him who sent Him. He did the Father's will and also waited for the Father's time (John 7:6).

Satan tempted the Lord to do something without God's word by asking Him to turn stones into bread. But the Lord answered and said that man shall live on every word of God (Matt. 4:4). He said many times that He only spoke what He had heard, and in John 5:30 He said, "I can do nothing from Myself." This means that He did not consider the self as His source. Satan always wants man to justify himself after God has already justified him. This is like Satan trying to persuade the Lord to declare that He was the Son of God after God had already declared this.

The crucifixion of the Lord was according to the will of God. He prayed in Gethsemane, "Not as I will, but as You will" (Matt. 26:39). "If this cannot pass away unless I drink it, Your will be done" (Matt. 26:42). At the end He said, "The cup which the Father has given Me, shall I not drink it?" (John 18:11). To be able to accept the cross is a victory. Not to be shaken by things inwardly or outwardly is a victory. Overcoming is having nothing of the flesh within, nothing of the world without, and nothing of Satan below. Throughout His life, the Lord did not allow the flesh to come into His living. He always put aside the flesh. The Lord was the first One from whom Satan could gain nothing. Neither the flesh nor the world had any ground in Him.

God Intending the Church to Live Out the Victory of Christ

God's salvation of man is to save him from the flesh, the world, and Satan. God wants us to refuse everything that is from the world, earth, self, flesh, and Satan. Satan attacks us through the world and flesh. Only those who are absolutely spiritual, who have absolutely refused the worldly system and the will of the flesh, will be attacked by Satan directly.

The cross of Christ needs the Body of Christ. If a sinner merely accepts the cross objectively, only he himself will gain something. However, if we accept the cross subjectively, God will gain something. The cross of Christ cuts off like a knife everything of the old creation, while His resurrection brings us into a new beginning.

The victory of Christ is seen in (1) the crucifixion which removes the whole old creation on the negative side, (2) the resurrection which brings in a new beginning on the positive side, and (3) the ascension which secures for Him the position of victory.

The church lives out Christ's victory on earth by the death, resurrection, and ascension of Christ. The cross should be planted in the center of our life. God wants us to be responsible for the cross' cutting off of that part of the old creation which is known to us. God does not want us to be responsible for that part of the old creation which is not known to us. ❧

(Afternoon, January 25)

WHO ARE GOD'S OVERCOMERS

Scripture Reading:
Revelation 2:7, 11, 17, 26; 3:5, 12, 21

The Failure of the Church

The reason that the church is on the earth is to maintain the victory of Christ on the cross and bind Satan in each locality as the Lord bound him on Calvary. On the cross the Lord has condemned Satan according to the law. Now God desires that the church execute this judgment on the earth.

Satan knows that the church will be involved in his defeat. This is why he persecutes and tries to deceive the church with his falsehood. He is a murderer and a liar. The church is not afraid of his angry countenance but of his smiling face. The Acts of the Apostles is the record of how the church passed through death into life. God used Satan's attack to display Christ's victory. However, the church gradually became degraded. For example, there were the falsehood of Ananias and Sapphira, the greediness of Simon, the admission of false brothers, the care of many for their own affairs, and the forsaking by many of Paul when he was in prison.

God's Search for Overcomers

After the failure of the church, God searched for a small number of people in the church to become His overcomers, those who would bear the responsibility which the church should have picked up but did not. God wanted a small number of faithful ones to represent the church and maintain the victory of Christ. In all of the seven ages of the church, there are God's overcomers. This line of overcomers has never been broken. The overcomers are not special people. The overcomers of God are a group of people who are one with God's original purpose.

The Principle of the Overcomers

According to the Bible, when God wants to do something, He first chooses a small number of people as a base and then works the same thing into the majority of the people. The record of the age of the patriarchs proves this principle is true. At that time, God chose men here and there in a scattered way. There were men like Abel, Enoch, Noah, and Abraham. From Abraham, the record went on to the Israelites; from the dispensation of the patriarchs, to the dispensation of the law; from the dispensation of the law, to the dispensation of grace; from the dispensation of grace, to the dispensation of the kingdom; and from the dispensation of the kingdom, to the new heaven and new earth. The kingdom is a precursor to the new heaven and new earth. The altar and the tabernacle of the dispensation of the law typify items of the dispensation of grace. This is the principle of God's work; it always goes from few to many.

Colossians 2:19 says, "And...holding the Head, out from whom all the Body, being richly supplied and knit together by means of the joints and sinews, grows with the growth of God."

"Joints" are for supply, while "sinews" are for the knitting together. The Head supplies and knits together the whole body through the joints and sinews. Only the overcomers can be the supplying joints and the connecting sinews.

Jerusalem typifies the church. Within Jerusalem, there was Mount Zion. One typifies the whole body of the church, while the other typifies the overcomers of the church. Jerusalem is large, while Zion is small. The stronghold of Jerusalem is Zion. Whenever there is something that has to do with God's heart desire, Zion is mentioned. Whenever there is something that has to do with the failures and sins of the Jews, Jerusalem is mentioned. God always allowed Jerusalem to be trodden down, but He always protected Zion. There is a New Jerusalem, but there never will be a new Zion, because Zion can never become old. Every time the Old Testament speaks of the relationship between Zion and Jerusalem, it shows us that the characteristics, the life, the blessing, and the establishment of Jerusalem come from Zion. In 1 Kings 8:1, the elders were in Jerusalem, and the ark of the covenant was in Zion. Psalm 51:18 says that God did good to Zion and built the walls of Jerusalem. Psalm 102:21 says that the name of the Lord was in Zion and that His praise was in Jerusalem. Psalm 128:5 says that the Lord blessed out of Zion and that the good was seen in Jerusalem. Psalm 135:21 says that the Lord dwelt at Jerusalem but that the Lord was to be blessed out of Zion. In Isaiah 41:27 the word was first announced to Zion and then preached to Jerusalem. Joel 3:17 says that when God dwelt in Zion, Jerusalem would be holy.

Today God is looking for the one hundred and forty-four thousand amidst the defeated church, who will stand on Mount Zion (Rev. 14). God always uses a small number of believers to pass on the flow of life to the church and to revive the church. As the Lord has done once before, so these overcomers have to pour out their blood before life can flow out to others. On behalf of the church, the overcomers take the stand of victory and also suffer tribulation and despising.

Thus, the overcomers of God need to give up what they consider as right. They have to pay the price and allow the cross to cut off all the old creation and deal with the gates of Hades (Matt. 16:18).

Are you willing to endure heartache to gain the heart of God? Are you willing to let yourself be defeated so that the Lord can be the Victor? When your obedience is fulfilled, God will deal with all disobedience (2 Cor. 10:6).

(Afternoon, January 26)

WHAT IS THE WORK OF THE OVERCOMER?

Scripture Reading:
Joshua 3:6, 8, 13, 15-17; 4:10-11, 15-18;
2 Corinthians 4:10-12

The Work of the Overcomer

In considering the overcomers, we need to pay attention to two things: (1) God chose a few persons to take the place of all the people who failed. (2) God made the few carry out God's command first, and then He worked the same thing into the majority.

God chose the Israelites to be a kingdom of priests among all people (Exo. 19:5-6), but they failed because they worshipped the golden calf at Mount Sinai. God then chose the sons of Levi, who had done His command, to be His overcomers to replace the Israelites as the priests (Exo. 32:15-29).

Originally God intended that the whole tribe of Israel be the priests. But because they worshipped the idol, God made the Levites to replace the Israelites as the priests.

God works on a few persons first. Then He works on the majority of the people through these few. Before God could deliver the Israelites, He first had to deliver Moses. God had to deliver

Moses out of Egypt before He could deliver the Israelites out of Egypt. God had to deal with David to gain him first, before He could deliver the Israelites from the hand of the Philistines and could make them a nation. All spiritual goals must be fulfilled by spiritual means. God had to deal with Moses and David to the extent that they would no longer try to fulfill God's will by their flesh or exercise their flesh to render God the help.

First God gained twelve people, then one hundred and twenty, and finally He established the church. God allows a few persons to take up the responsibility which the majority should but would not. The principle of the overcomers is for God to allow a few persons to do something that results in blessing for the majority. He makes a few persons to stand in death so that the majority will receive life. God plants the cross into their heart for them to experience the principle of the cross in their family and their environment. The result of this is that life is poured into others. God needs channels of life in order to pour out life to others.

Standing in the Place of Death that Others May Receive Life

God put the priests in the place of death so that the Israelites would have a way to the land of life. The priests were the first ones to go into the water and the last ones to come up out of the water. They were the overcomers of God. Today God is seeking for a group of people who, like the priests of old, step into the water, that is, walk into death first. They are willing to be dealt with by the cross first, to stand in the place of death in order that the church will find the way of life. God must first put us in the place of death before others can receive life. The overcomers of God are the pioneers of God.

The priests could not do much by themselves; they merely bore the ark. They had to bear the ark of the covenant and go down into the midst of the water. We have to let Christ be the center, to put on Christ, and to go down to the water. The feet of the priests were standing on the riverbed while their shoulders were bearing the ark. They were standing in death, while lifting up Christ.

The bottom of the river is the position of death; it is not comfortable, attractive, or restful. They were not sitting there, nor lying there, but standing there. If I live in my temper, Christ cannot live in others. If I stand at the bottom of the river, others will cross over the Jordan victoriously. Death works in me, but life works in others. If I die in submitting to God, life will work in others to make them also submit to God. The death of Christ works His life into us. Without death, there is no life.

To bear the ark of the covenant at the bottom of the river is a great suffering. They needed to be very careful. If they were not careful, the holy God would destroy them. They stood there watching the Israelites crossing one by one. Yet they were set to be last. The apostle said, "God has set forth us the apostles last"; "we have become as the offscouring of the world, the scum of all things, until now" (1 Cor. 4:9, 13). He wished all would believe in the gospel but not be like him with chains on his hands (Acts 26:29). Do I want a good report, an easy life, or sympathy? Or do I want the church of God to gain life? May we be able to pray, "Lord, let me die so that others can gain life." God has said clearly that this is not an easy matter. Yet only in this way will God accomplish His eternal plan.

Before they could come out, they waited at the bottom of the river for all of God's people to cross over. We cannot come out of death before the kingdom comes. Eventually Joshua commanded, saying, "Come up out of the Jordan" (Josh. 4:17). Our triumphant Joshua will tell us to come up out of the water. This will happen at the beginning of the kingdom.

Many people are not disobedient; they are merely not obedient enough. It is not that they have not paid the price, but that they have not paid enough. It is not that they would not spend the money, or that they would not raise an army, but what they do is not adequate (Luke 14:25-35). Without going through the cross, one cannot reach Gethsemane. Without dealing with the cross, one cannot say, "Your will be done." Many people like the calling of Abraham, yet they do not like the consecration on Mount Moriah.

Have you ever envied others' easy living? God has put us at the river bottom in order that we would be His overcomers. He put us in chains in order that others can receive the gospel. Death works in me but life in others. This is the only channel of life. The life that flows into us has passed through two pipes, Paul and Martin Luther. The Lord's death first fills us with life, and then this life flows to others (2 Cor. 4:10-12).

The work of God's overcomer is to stand upon Christ's death so that others can gain life. The words of the Bible must first be realized by us before we can preach them. The light of the truth must first become life to us before it will become light to others. God makes His overcomers first see a truth and confirm such truth before He gains some others to obey this truth. Truth must first be constituted in us and become a part of our being. We ourselves must first have the experience of faith, prayer, and consecration before we can tell others what faith, prayer, and consecration are. Otherwise, we will only have the terms without the content. God wants us to go through death first after which He will give others life. We first must pass through the sufferings and the pain before others can have the life. To learn God's truth, one must stand at the bottom of the river first. The reason the church cannot gain the victory by crossing over to the good land is that there is a shortage of priests who will stand in the bottom of the Jordan. Those who stand in the bottom of the Jordan will create a seeking heart in others. If a truth is deeply constituted in us, it will attract others to pursue the truth. Today, many of God's truths need to be constituted in man. When we allow a truth to be constituted in us, we are allowing the Body of Christ to grow one more inch. The overcomers are those who receive life from above to supply the Body. ✱

(Afternoon, January 27)

THE EXPERIENCE OF THE OVERCOMERS

Who are God's overcomers? The overcomers are the ones who allow their "self" to remain in the place of death in order that others might have the life. These ones are like the priests who bore the ark through the Jordan, who themselves stood in the place of death in order that the people of God could pass through. What does death here signify? What does it mean to stand in the place of death? This is a very crucial point; it has to do with the going on of God's people. This is the one thing that God is concerned with the most today. For this reason, it should also be the one thing that we are concerned with the most.

The truths in the Bible are not put together in bits and pieces. Behind every truth, there is something living. The letter of the truth is dead; it does not have life. In order for the truth to become living, there is the need for a living spirit. Many truths in the Bible are read, preached, and believed by men. But these truths must be experienced, dealt with, and transformed into life before they can become powerful to us. Many people think that those people who are more intelligent will receive more scriptural truths than others or will understand more of the things of God. This is absolutely wrong. Spiritual truths are not limited by our natural wisdom. Many people think that they can help others by acquiring something by their own strength and wisdom and conveying the same to others. Actually, this will not give life to others.

John 1 says that the Lord is the light of life. Many people think that as long as they understand this truth and preach this truth, everything will be all right. They think that the truth is the truth and that it is not necessary that it has to have anything to do with the person himself. But this is not God's way. His way is first to constitute the truth in a man, so that the truth becomes part of his constitution before he can preach this truth to others. A man must be dealt with, cut open, and saturated by the truth in a deep way before he can convey this truth to others. If a truth has never gone through God's constituting work, it will not produce any effect on man.

Let me give you a few illustrations.

Faith

The first item is faith. What is faith? It does not mean that you know about faith on Saturday and then preach it on the Lord's Day. You may have the letter but not have seen the thing itself. This is like talking to primitive people about the electric light. They may know the term but never have seen the thing itself. They may act like they understand. But in fact, they do not know what the thing is.

Therefore, God must first deal with you through matters; you first must be dealt with in the matter of faith and allow God's faith to be constituted in you before you can convey to others what is constituted in you. Only then can you render help to others. Only when death works in you will life work in others.

Prayer

Next, let us consider prayer. Teaching others to pray is not a matter of preparing or composing some doctrines on prayer. God has to take you through many environments before He can teach you the lesson on prayer. Only after many such experiences will you be able to tell others the way to pray. In everything, you must first be God's experiment.

Real prayer requires more strength than I exert in preaching. Many times we think that as long as we can deliver a good message, everything will be all right. But we have to realize that it is only after we have prayed thoroughly that our message will flow into others.

What we have mentioned above is the principle of God. This principle states that one must first go through sufferings and pay the price to have the experience before he can communicate the truth to others. Such ones are the overcomers according to God's desire.

Consecration

Let us again take up the matter of consecration as an illustration. What is absolute consecration? The Bible speaks of this, and men talk about this. But many only have the letters without having seen the thing itself. This is like a person reading a dictionary; he can read the words in the dictionary, but he does not know what the words indicate. The same is true with the church of God. One day when God compares your family, your work, your possessions, your career, and your loved ones with Christ, you will realize what it is to live for the Lord. What will you choose? Will you choose Christ or something else? Will you bargain with God? No truth can be acquired without paying a price. I am afraid that many people have learned the truth but do not have any experience of it.

The Need for the Truth to Be Constituted in the Workers

How much of the truth in you has never been constituted? How much of what you know has never been realized in you? From this we see that men today do not even know what obedience is, what prayer is, and what faith is. There is no short cut to learning God's truth. The seed determines what the plant eventually will be. How a worker is, determines how the ones he works on will be. If you are not a serious person, the fruit you bear will surely not be serious. If you are a sober person, the fruit you bear will be sober. The kind of person you are determines the kind of fruit you will produce. I have seen men preaching the doctrine of "dying with Christ," "living with Christ," and "ascending with Christ," but the person himself had nothing to do with the spiritual things he was speaking of.

Once I asked Miss Barber how one can produce the sense of the need of life within others and generate a hunger within them. She replied, "On the one hand, this matter depends on God. But on the other hand, there are things that the workers themselves have to be responsible for. Let us not consider God's side for now.

On the worker's side, whether or not he can create in others a spiritual hunger does not depend on what he says but on what he is. When an advanced one is put together with one who has not made much progress, that one will spontaneously realize his backwardness. When an obedient one is put together with a disobedient one, the disobedient one will spontaneously recognize his own disobedience. In the same way, when a holy one is put side by side with an unholy one, the unholy one will spontaneously realize his own unholiness. If you are not that type of person, you will not be able to produce that type of hunger in others."

The nature which we have inherited in regeneration is very prone to imitate. If you put it in front of holiness, it will spontaneously incline toward holiness. If you put it in front of obedience, it will spontaneously learn to obey. We should be a group of people who take the lead to grow before God. Today God is attracting others to the shore through the experience of the cross and the endurance of sufferings in the life of the overcomers. The ones who entered the water first were the priests; they took the lead to stand in the death water. The overcomers are the pioneers; they open up a way in the midst of darkness and take the lead into death. Only by doing this will they be able to help others to go through in the same way.

Believers in the past mostly stumbled their way through. But believers today are told of the way others have stumbled through. All they have to do today is to obey and allow the truth already released to be constituted in their very being. These are the ones who have the ark on their shoulders, whose feet are on the earth, and who are standing firmly on the ground of death. Only by bearing Christ on our shoulder in this way can we be God's overcomers. If God cannot gain us as such a group of overcomers, He will have to find someone else.

Every time the cross comes upon you, or every time God deals with you, are you willing to accept the dealing, or will you run away from it? This is the crucial question today. ❋

(Afternoon, January 28)

THE SELECTION OF THE OVERCOMERS

Scripture Reading:
Judges 6:1-6, 11-35; 7:1-8, 19-25; 8:1-4

Now we come to the matter of selecting the overcomers, of how to separate the overcomers from the non-overcomers.

Numbers says that every male of the Israelites from twenty years old and upward had to be a soldier to go forth to war for the Lord. At the time of the Judges, the Israelites had failed. In order for God to deliver them all, He had to select three hundred men who would fight the battle which the others should but did not fight. The others had failed and would not fight for Jehovah anymore. Many people know how to keep the faith and finish the course, yet they do not know how to fight the good fight.

How to Be an Overcomer—Gideon

Realizing Oneself to Be the Least: Knowing the Self

It is easy to be humble before God, but it is very difficult to be humble before man in comparison with others. Saying, "I am the least" is easy, but saying, "I am the least in my father's house" is not easy. Saying, "My family is poor" is easy, but saying, "My family is poor in Manasseh" is not easy (Judg. 6:15). The overcomers do not see the shining on their own faces, though others may see it. All those who see the shining on their own faces through a mirror are not overcomers. Though David was anointed, he still considered himself a dog. The overcomers have the reality of an overcomer rather than the name of an overcomer.

Seeing the Heavenly Vision: Seeing the Lord

No one can work without seeing a vision. If one has the vision, though he may encounter difficulties, he will still reach his goal. When we have the Lord's word, we can cross to the other side. When we have the vision, our footsteps will be steadfast in our work.

Seeing and Not Disobeying the Vision: Responding to the Lord's Call by Offering the Sacrifices

We need to offer up ourselves, even what we regard to be the least, to the hand of God. It does not matter whether we see ourselves as big or as small. If we do not put ourselves in the hand of God, both are equally futile. All living sacrifices that are according to God's will are acceptable to God. The overcomers were called by God. Have you heard and answered the call to the overcomers in Revelation 2 and 3?

Tearing Down the Idols: Making an Outward Testimony

After one has consecrated himself in his heart, he still needs to tear down the idols as an outward testimony. We need to be aware of ourselves, our family, and those with whom we have contact. Anything that occupies equal standing with God should be torn down. Only those who have seen God know what an idol is. Only those who have seen the Angel of God, who is the Lord, know that anything besides the Lord is an idol. Only after one has seen the Angel of God will he realize that the wooden image is not God. The sacrifice on the rock (Judg. 6:21) is for the individual, but the sacrifice on the altar (v. 24) is for the multitude.

After having passed through these four steps, the Holy Spirit came upon Gideon. The filling of the Holy Spirit does not come as a result of prayer for power. When a man stands in the proper condition, the Holy Spirit will come upon him.

The blowing of the trumpet (v. 34) is a call for others to join the ranks of the overcomers. Overcomers should not act independently. We should separate ourselves from the defeated ones, but we should not separate ourselves from the other overcomers.

How to Select the Overcomers—The Three Hundred Men

The First Selection

The first selection resulted in twenty-two thousand people leaving. They left because (1) they wanted to glorify themselves. We are willing to give up our life but not to give up our glory. Not only do we have to overcome Satan, we have to overcome ourselves as well. God wants only those who will work for Him without boasting about it. After working for God, we should merely say, "We are unprofitable slaves" (Luke 17:10). We should forget how much we have plowed, how many sheep we have shepherded. God cannot divide His glory between Him and us. If we still expect anything for ourselves, we will be eliminated. These ones also left because (2) they were fearful and afraid (Josh. 7:3). Whoever is fearful and afraid will be asked to leave. One must not love himself but must endure suffering. The greatest suffering is not material but spiritual. Whoever wants to glorify himself and is fearful and afraid will be eliminated. Overcoming does not depend on the number of people but on knowing God.

The Second Selection

The selection this time was based on a very small matter, that of drinking. A small matter always exposes what we are. In those days both the Jews and the Arabs carried their luggage on their backs when they traveled. There were two ways to drink water along the way. One was to put down the luggage and kneel, bowing down to the ground to drink with the mouth. The other was to leave the luggage on the back and drink by putting the hand to the mouth. The latter was done for the sake of saving time for the journey and also for guarding oneself from robbers. Among the ten thousand, nine thousand and seven hundred drank with their mouths directly to the water, while three hundred drank by putting water in their hand to the mouth. Those who drank directly with their mouths were eliminated by God. Those who drank by bringing water in their hand to the mouth were selected by God. A person who has the chance to indulge himself but who will not do so is one who has been dealt with by the cross. This kind of person can be used by God. God can only use those who are willing to be unconditionally dealt with by the cross.

The three conditions by which God selects the overcomers are: (1) being absolute for God's glory, (2) being afraid of nothing, and (3) allowing the cross to deal with the self. One can judge for himself if he is an overcomer. God will test us, and we will be exposed as to whether or not we are overcomers. Only those who know the victory of the cross will be able to maintain the victory of the cross.

The Oneness of the Overcomers

God gave Gideon three hundred men and made them one body. Individual victory is not proper. Gideon and those three hundred men moved together and acted in one accord. All of their flesh was cut off, so they could be one. This is the oneness in the Spirit and a living in the Body. The record in the New Testament is a record of meetings rather than a record of working.

The Result

The three hundred men fought the battle, yet the whole congregation chased the enemy. The three hundred labored, yet the whole congregation reaped the harvest. When we overcome, the whole body is revived. To stand at the bottom of the river is not for ourselves, but for the whole body. "I…fill up on my part that which is lacking of the afflictions of Christ in my flesh for His Body, which is the church" (Col. 1:24). To be an overcomer, we also have to suffer the murmurings of the people, in the same way that Gideon suffered the murmurings of the men from Ephraim. Gideon not only defeated the Midianites from without but also defeated the Midianites from within. Only this kind of person can continue to overcome. They were "weary yet pursuing" (Judg. 8:4b). ❦

(Afternoon, January 29)

THE OVERCOMER'S PRAYER

Scripture Reading:
Matthew 18:18; Ephesians 6:12-13; 1:20-22; 2:6;
Mark 11:23-24

Authoritative Prayer—Praying with Authority

To be God's overcomer, one has to learn to pray with authority by exercising Christ's authority. In the Bible prayer is not merely a petition but a representation of authority. Prayer is to command with authority.

God's overcomer must first be faithful to deny the self, the world, and Satan. We should first allow God to defeat us by the cross, that is we should allow ourselves to be defeated before God. Second, we must know how to apply Christ's authority. We should exercise Christ's authority to defeat Satan, that is, we should win the victory over Satan. Authoritative prayers are not petitions but commands. There are two kinds of prayer: petitioning prayers and commanding prayers. Isaiah 45:11 says, "Command Me." We can command God to do something. This is a commanding prayer.

Commanding prayer begins from Christ's ascension. Christ's death and resurrection solved God's four big problems. The death of Christ solved all the problems in Adam. His resurrection granted us a new position. His ascension seated us in the heavens, far above all rule, authority, power, lordship, and every name that is named, not only in this age, but also in that which is to come. Ephesians 1 refers to Christ's ascension far above all principality and power. Chapter two refers to the fact that we are also seated in the heavens with Him. Therefore, as Christ is far above all rule and authority, we also are far above all rule and authority.

Ephesians 1 tells us that Christ's position is in the heavens. Chapter two tells us of our position in Christ, which is that we are seated with Christ in the heavenlies. Chapter six tells us what we do in the heavenlies. We are to sit in the heavenlies and pray by issuing commanding prayers with the authority of Christ's victory.

A common prayer is one that prays from earth to heaven. A commanding prayer is one that prays from heaven to earth. Matthew 6 is a prayer of petition; it is upward. Ephesians 6 is a commanding prayer; it is downward. We are sitting in the heavenlies issuing prayers of command. *Amen* in Hebrew means "definitely so." This is a command. Satan, at the beginning of all battles, tries to dislodge our position as victors in the heavenlies. To battle means to fight for our position, while to overcome means to occupy our position. In Christ we sit in the heavenly position and are able to pray with authoritative prayer.

The words "for this reason" in Mark 11:24 indicate that verse 23 is also on prayer. But verse 23 does not tell us to pray to God. It merely says, "Whoever says to this mountain," that is, commands the mountain. It is not a direct speaking to God, but it is still a prayer, a prayer of command. It is not to ask God to do something but to exercise God's authority to deal with the mountain, the things that hinder us. Absolute faith comes out of absolute knowledge of God's will. Only with this faith can we speak to the mountain. We command what God has already commanded and decide what God has already decided. We have faith through having a full knowledge of God's will.

The Relationship between Authoritative Prayers and the Overcomers

The one who sits on the throne is God, who is the Lord. The one who is under the throne is the enemy. Prayer unites us to God. The overcoming ones, the reigning and ruling ones, know how to pray and exercise the authority of God's throne. (This authority of God's throne governs the world.) We may turn to the throne and apply the authority there to call a brother to come. (Hudson Taylor did this before.) In order to rule over the church, the world, and the authority in the heavenlies, the overcomers have to exercise the authority of the throne. In England about ten years ago, there were some brothers who had applied the authority of God's throne to govern the political changes. This is to rule over the nations. Spiritual battle is not only defensive but also offensive. We will not only rule over the nations but also over Hades and all rule, authority, power, and lordship. May God grant us to know how to exercise Christ's authority. All things are under Christ's feet. He is the Head of the church. When we exercise Christ's authority, all things will be under our feet also.

Matthew 18:18-19 refers to praying. "On earth" and "in the heavens" in verse 19 show us that the prayer in verse 18 is a command. This praying is an execution, not a petition. It is a binding and a loosing, not a petitioning for God to bind and loose. There are two aspects to this commanding prayer. The first is to bind. We should bind the brothers and sisters who do not behave properly in the meetings. We should bind the world that frustrates the work. We should bind the demons and the evil spirits, and we should bind Satan and all his work. We can be kings and rule over all things. Whenever something goes wrong in the world or among the brothers, it is time for us to rule as kings. The second aspect to a commanding prayer is to loose. We should be those who can loose others. We should loose the brothers who are withdrawn. We should loose the brothers who need to free themselves for the work. We should loose men's money for God. We should loose the truth of God. We are ambassadors sent by God. On this earth, we should enjoy our right of "foreign diplomatic immunity." We can call on heaven to dominate this earth. ❦

(Afternoon, January 30)

WHAT GOD'S OVERCOMERS SHOULD DO AT THE END OF THIS AGE

Scripture Reading:
Genesis 3:14-15; Revelation 12:1-11

The two passages we read today correspond with each other. One is in the beginning of the Bible while the other is at the end.

In Genesis 3 we have (1) the serpent, (2) the woman, and (3) the seed. In Revelation 12 we have (1) the serpent, (2) the woman, and (3) the man-child.

God's Pronouncement on the Serpent

Genesis 3 covers God's pronouncement on man and on the serpent after the fall. It also covers God's redemption. "Upon thy belly shalt thou go" means God restricted Satan's work to the earth; he can no longer work throughout the universe. "And dust shalt thou eat all the days of thy life" means God restricted Satan to feed on the man of dust. God ordained that all the descendants of Adam be the food of Satan.

"The woman" was the mother of all living. Hence, the woman represents all the living ones whom God intends to save.

"The seed of the woman" means Christ. When Christ was on the earth, He bruised the serpent's head. The head is the vital part of a body. The Lord bruised the vital power of Satan.

The serpent bruising His heel means Satan doing his work behind Christ's back. After Christ bruised the serpent's head, He went on, while the serpent worked behind His back. This has always been the way he works in the believers—behind their back.

"The seed of the woman" refers to the individual Christ; it also refers to the corporate Christ. Those who participate in Christ's resurrection are the seed of the woman. The Lord was born of a woman and is without the Adamic nature. Likewise, the regenerated new man in the believers does not have Adam's nature in it. Christ is the Son of God, and the new man is also the son of God. Christ is not out of the flesh, neither is the new man out of the flesh nor out of the will of man.

Beginning from Genesis 3, both God and man set their hope on the seed of the woman. Satan also paid much attention to the seed of the woman. That is why he tried to stir up Herod to kill the Lord, why he tempted the Lord in the wilderness, and why he persecuted Him during the three and a half years. But in all these situations, the Lord overcame.

The Overcomers Dealing with the Serpent

Revelation 4 through 11 is one section. Chapter fifteen to the end is another section. Chapters twelve through fourteen are inserted as a footnote for the previous chapters; they do not form part of the main text. Chapter twelve is a continuation of chapters two and three. These two chapters mention "overcoming" seven times, while chapter twelve says "they overcame him." Chapters two and three mention God's calling of the overcomers at the time when most of the church has failed, while chapter twelve tells what these overcomers are and what they do. Revelation 2:27 says that the overcomers will rule the nations with an iron rod, while 12:5 says that the man-child will rule over the nations with an iron rod. The overcomers in the church are the man-child. The man-child is corporate, composed of the "brothers" in verses 10 and 11.

The Lord purposely calls Satan the "ancient serpent" here to remind us of the record in Genesis 3.

In Revelation 12 the woman who brought forth the man-child is Jerusalem. This does not refer only to the earthly Jerusalem but also to the heavenly Jerusalem. The Bible tells us that God is our Father, the Lord is our elder Brother, and Jerusalem is our mother (Gal. 4:26).

The sun, the moon, and the twelve stars are consistent with the dream of Joseph. Hence, these things refer to the Israelites. Jerusalem is the center for the Israelites. Hence, this woman must mean Jerusalem.

This woman is the Jerusalem in chapters twenty-one and twenty-two. This city is composed of all the saved ones in the Old and the New Testaments, who have the life of Christ in them. The woman before the bringing forth of the man-child is a type of the church. The woman after the bringing forth of the man-child is a type of the Israelites. Before the bringing forth of the man-child, the description was concerning the things in the heavens—the sun, the moon, and the stars. After the bringing forth of the man-child, the description is concerning her condition on earth—fleeing to the wilderness.

The woman typifies the many sons whom God has saved. They will be very much persecuted by the enemy; the woman will suffer under the serpent. They should fight for themselves but because they cannot do this, God will raise up some overcomers from among them to fight for them. These overcomers will rule over the nations with an iron rod and will have a special place in the kingdom. When they are raptured to heaven, Satan will be cast down, and they will take back the serpent's place in heaven. When they are on earth, Satan will withdraw. When they are in heaven, Satan will be cast down. To overcome means to recover the lost ground. The man-child overcomes on behalf of the mother. This means that the overcomers overcome on behalf of the church. At the end times, God is looking for the overcomers to end the battle in heaven. God's "salvation and the power and the kingdom of our God and the authority of His Christ" (Rev. 12:10) will be brought to heaven by them. As a result, the serpent will no longer have a place in heaven. Wherever the overcomers go, Satan will have to withdraw.

The Weapons of the Overcomers

These overcomers overcome the enemy by the following things:

The Blood of the Lamb

First, the blood of Christ is poured out, signifying that the life of the flesh is poured out. Through this, Satan will not be able to do anything to us. The food of Satan is dust; he can only work within a life of the flesh. Second, the blood of Christ deals with the attack of Satan. We are protected under the blood of Christ from the attack of Satan, in the same way that the Israelites were protected under the blood of the Passover. The blood satisfies God's righteousness; it signifies death. Therefore, Satan cannot attack us. Third, the blood of Christ answers Satan's accusations.

The Word of Testimony

All the works of Satan in the church are to overthrow the testimony. The church is the lampstand, and the lampstand is a testimony. Satan wants to overthrow the church in order to overthrow the testimony. The testimony spoken of here refers especially to the testimony against Satan. When the Lord was tempted, He said three sentences which were testimonies directed at Satan. We also should declare a testimony against Satan. Satan may say to us, "You are weak." But we should say to him that the power of the Lord is perfected in weakness (2 Cor. 12:9). We should exercise the victory of Christ by applying God's Word. The blood speaks of the victory of Christ. A testimony is an application of the victory of Christ with the Word of God.

Not Loving One's Life

We should sacrifice our body and our life and have no pity on ourselves. We should "consider my life of no account as if precious to myself" (Acts 20:24). By the blood and the word of our testimony, we should not fear death but should fight until we overcome. Such men will fulfill the pronouncement of Genesis 3:15.

The dragon wants to devour the man-child which is about to be delivered. This is the reason we have persecutions and sufferings. These persecutions and sufferings force us to become the man-child, and cause us to be among the first to be raptured—the first rapture. The first rapture is not only a blessing but a responsibility. Whoever has a place for the dragon in his heart will be persecuted by the dragon; he will go through the tribulation. Whoever does not have a place for the dragon in his heart will step on the head of the dragon. The serpent corrupted the woman. This is why there is the need for the seed of the woman to bruise him. God will not defeat the serpent by Himself. God needs the overcomers to defeat him. May we be part of the overcomers. ❦

(Afternoon, January 31)
Spoken by Watchman Nee
Recorded by Witness Lee in Shanghai

4

MINISTERING TO THE HOUSE OR TO GOD?

"Yet they shall minister in My sanctuary,
having oversight at the gates of the house
and ministering in the house.
They shall slaughter the burnt offering and
the sacrifice for the people, and they shall stand
before them to minister to them."
Ezekiel 44:11

"...they shall come near to Me to minister to Me;
and they shall stand before Me
to present to Me the fat and the blood,
declares the Lord Jehovah."
Ezekiel 44:15b

Scripture Reading:
Ezekiel 44:9-26, 28, 31; Luke 17:7-10

These two portions of the Word show us two different attitudes that are displayed before God. Before we look into these matters using the Word with the shining of God's light, I want the brothers and sisters to know what are our responsibilities and what is God's continual focus in the church in this age.

Brothers and sisters, let me ask something very frankly. Are we really ministering to the believers or to Him? Is the focus of our work really on the work or on the Lord? There is a great difference.

Ministering to the house is extremely different from ministering to Jesus Christ. We can see many today ministering and serving, but they are only in the outer court. They have not come near to the table. Oh, many are ministering to the house and not to the Lord. The ministering that the Lord is after—the ministering that He is continually after—is to minister to Him. His desire is not for us to do His work. Laboring is certainly important, plowing the fields is important, and feeding the cattle is also important, but the Lord does not look at these things. Rather, He is after the ministering to God and the serving of God. He wants His slaves to minister to Him and to serve Him. Oh, how happy are those who are able to minister to Him.

Now I want to mention the difference between these two kinds of ministering. Let us search these two portions of the Word. We are not here to expound the Scriptures. The expounding of the Scriptures has become the trap to many spiritual believers. There is really no matter that has so damaged the believers as the expounding of the Scriptures. I am speaking of the spiritual believers here. We always assume that as long as we can find two similar verses in the Scriptures, then we can expound them. No. There is no such thing! Today we will first learn a lesson and then study the lesson. Before we study the lesson, we must first learn the lesson and know how to minister to God. We must first meet the One who wrote the Book before we can read the words. We must first know Him before we can know His Book. If we put the Bible as the top priority, we are failures. Therefore, from the beginning we want to declare that we are not here to expound the Scriptures; rather, we are here to learn a lesson. As such we are using these two portions of the Word to proclaim what we should have experienced and what we have experienced.

Ezekiel 44:11, 15-16 says, "Yet they shall minister in My sanctuary, having oversight at the gates of the house and ministering in the house. They shall slaughter the burnt offering and the sacrifice for the people, and they shall stand before them to minister to them....But the Levitical priests, the sons of Zadok, that kept the charge of My sanctuary when the children of Israel went astray from

Me, they shall come near to Me to minister to Me; and they shall stand before Me to present to Me the fat and the blood, declares the Lord Jehovah, It is they who will enter into My sanctuary, and it is they who will come near to My table to minister to Me, and they will keep My charge." You see that verse 11 is very different from verses 15 and 16. There is a basic difference between them. Verse 11 speaks of ministering to the house. Verses 15 and 16 speak of ministering to "Me"—that is, the ministering to Jehovah. In Hebrew, the same word for ministering is used in both of these verses. According to God there were two groups of Levites. Although all were Levites belonging to God and to one tribe, the majority among them were only worthy to minister to the house. Yet there was a small minority, who were not only Levites but also the sons of Zadok, who could minister to "Me"—that is, minister to Jehovah.

Brothers and sisters, do you know what it is to minister to the house and what it is to minister to Jehovah? Do you know the difference between these two kinds of ministering? Many say that there is nothing better than ministering to the house! They seem to say, "You see me doing my best to make my work expand, to strive for the kingdom, to work in the Lord's name, to bear the responsibility to help the church, and to earnestly endeavor to be the slave of the brothers. I do my best to render help to the brothers and sisters. I rush about to different places so as to make the church flourish and the work prosper." Many feel that it would be wonderful if they could save sinners and ask them to join the church, thereby causing the church to grow in numbers. But I say this is merely ministering to the house. As far as God is concerned, besides this kind of ministering, there is another kind of ministering. In God's eyes, not only is there the ministry to the house; there is also a better ministry. We are not only ministering before the Lord but also to the Lord. Here there is not only the ministering in the house, but there is also the ministering before the table. We are not only ministering before the Lord; rather, we are ministering to the Lord. This is a very different matter. These two are extremely different from each other. There is no similarity between them.

If you know the difference here, you will see what the Lord is after and what He has always been seeking. Brothers and sisters, please do not be mistaken. To minister to the Lord does not mean that you neglect the house. Rather, what I am saying is that there is not only ministering to the house, but there is something deeper, which is ministering to the Lord. There are many who only know how to minister to the house and not to the Lord.

Let me ask you a few questions. Brothers, what are you preaching the gospel for? You desire to help prosper the work, but what is that really for? You rush to different places to labor, but what is that really for? I especially want to speak to the brothers and sisters who are co-workers. What are you really doing here? Do you hope that more can hear the gospel? I only mention the good things. I will not mention those things which are of a lower standard. No doubt it is good to preach the gospel. It is also good to save the sinners and help the brothers and sisters make progress. No doubt you have done your best to be very faithful to preach and perfect. However, your eyes are only set on the brothers and sisters. This is ministering to the house. Since you are ministering before people, you are ministering to them and not to the Lord. This does not mean that those who minister to the Lord will not do these things. Those who minister to the Lord will also do these things, but their one goal is to be for the Lord. They treasure men absolutely for the Lord's sake. Hence, their focus is not only on men. If you come to the Lord's presence, focusing only on Him, you will spontaneously be able to minister to the brothers also. This is a big difference.

In the following sections, we will see the basic difference between ministering to the Lord and ministering to the house. Then we will see how to minister to the Lord and how to minister to the house. Finally, we will see the requirements of one who ministers to the Lord. These are three matters we will mention.

THE DIFFERENCE BETWEEN MINISTERING TO THE HOUSE AND MINISTERING TO THE LORD

We must see clearly that outwardly there may not be much difference between ministering to the house and ministering to the

Lord. You may try your best to render help to the brothers, to diligently save the sinners, and to labor much in the service to manage the church. On top of these, you may do your best to admonish others to read the Bible and pray. You may have suffered much and have been persecuted. You may do everything. But there is a basic question: What is your motivation for doing this? The question hinges on whether or not the Lord occupies the first place in your heart. When you rise up early in the morning to minister to the brothers and sisters, do you say, "O Lord, today I am doing this once again for Your sake"? Or do you first remember that this is your duty, and you do it because this is what you should do? If this is the case, it is altogether out of necessity, and it is not for the Lord. You only saw your brothers; you did not see the Lord. Your motive tells everything about your situation. Your situation hinges on why you do things.

Let me tell you very frankly: the work has areas that are appealing to the flesh. Brothers, let us take, for example, a person who is active by nature. It is his nature to speak a great deal. If you ask him to go to the countryside to preach the gospel, run to and fro from one village to another, and speak here and there, he is very happy. Why do you think he does this? He is basically an active person who loves to speak. I can tell you frankly that he is not doing this for the Lord because many times he is not able to do the things he does not like, even though the Lord really wants him to. According to his nature, he likes to preach the gospel; so he is happy to do it and feels that he is ministering to the Lord. Actually, he is ministering to the house. Brothers and sisters, there is a big difference here! In the Lord's work there are areas which are interesting, adventurous, and attractive to the flesh! When you give messages, many flock to hear you. When you read a portion of the Bible, everyone comments that you have done a good job. When you preach the gospel, many are saved through you. This is really lovely and appealing to you. Just consider how interesting this is.

If I am doing housework, busying myself from morning till evening; if I am a worker in a factory, listening to the sound of machines from morning till evening; if I am an office worker, handling papers and letters from morning till evening; or if I am someone's maid, cleaning tables, mopping floors, and cooking for others from morning till evening, I might consider this to be meaningless! But if I could be free from these things to do the Lord's work, how good it would be! A sister may think it is dull to stay home and take care of the children, to be someone's wife, and to do all the household chores! If she could be set free to speak of spiritual things here and speak of the Lord's things there, how good it would be! But this is the attraction of the flesh and is not spiritual. It is solely for the pleasure of the self.

Oh, may we see that much of the labor and ministering before God is not ministering to Him. The Bible tells us that there was a group of Levites who were busily ministering in the house, but they were only ministering to the house, not to God. Ministering to the house is very similar to ministering to the Lord. Outwardly, there is almost no difference. Those Levites were in the house preparing the peace offerings and burnt offerings. This was a wonderful work. Suppose an Israelite wanted to worship God and offer up a peace offering and burnt offering, but he could not drag in the cattle or sheep. The Levites would help him drag in the animals and slay them. How good this was! They helped someone else be close to the Lord and know the Lord! Even today, it is a wonderful work to lead a sinner to turn or help a believer advance. While the Levites worked, they were very busy and their whole body was sweating. They helped others to carry out the offering of the cattle and sheep. Both the peace offering and burnt offering typify Christ. This means that they exerted their energy to bring others to the Lord. It is so wonderful that some could be brought to know the Lord. We know that the peace offering concerns the relationship between a sinner and the Lord, and the burnt offering concerns the relationship between a believer and the Lord. The peace offering speaks of a sinner's drawing near to the Lord, while the burnt offering speaks of the consecration of a believer. In the Levites' work, not only were sinners brought to believe in the Lord, but believers were also brought to consecrate themselves. How wonderful this work was. This was not a false work; it was altogether genuine. God knew their work. They were truly rendering help to others in offering up the peace offerings and burnt offerings. They were truly saving and helping men; they labored very hard. Nevertheless, God said they were not ministering to Him.

Brothers and sisters, please remember that ministering to the Lord is much deeper than leading men to the Lord. Ministering to the Lord is also much deeper than leading believers to consecrate themselves to the Lord. Ministering to the Lord is one step further than leading men to the Lord and leading believers to consecrate themselves to the Lord. In God's eyes, leading men to the Lord and leading believers to consecrate themselves to the Lord are merely ministering to the house. Ministering to the Lord is something deeper. What do you see before God? Do you only see the need for the salvation of sinners? Do you only see the need to render help for the progress of believers? Or do you see something deeper? I am not here to save sinners; neither am I here to render help to believers. Can you say this? I fear very much that many would say, "If saving sinners and rendering help to the believers is not my work, what shall I do? I will have nothing to do." Friends, besides these, do you have other work? Oh, with many this is all they have. Many say, "If I did not do the work of helping and saving others, what would I do?" Apart from these things, they have nothing to do. Their work is confined to the house. If you take away these things, they will have nothing left to do.

Brothers and sisters, if you knew the heavy burden within me, you would know the goal of God. God is not after the outward, lively ministering. God is not after the salvation of sinners. God is not after gaining men or helping believers to be more spiritual or more advanced. God has only one goal: to have men belong absolutely to "Me." In other words, He wants us to be before "My" presence and minister to "Me." God's unique goal is not in so many things. Rather, it is in "Me."

I say again, I am not afraid of bothering people. What I fear most in my heart is that many will come out to preach the gospel to help men, save sinners, and perfect the believers, yet not minister to the Lord! The goal of many so-called ministries to the Lord is none other than serving their own likes and pleasures. It is unbearable for them to be confined. They are energetic and must run around and be active in order to be happy! Although outwardly they are ministering to sinners and the brothers, inwardly they are ministering to their flesh! If they do not do this, they are not happy. Truly they are altogether not after the Lord's pleasure. It seems that I am giving you a hard time, but this is the truth. Please remember, there are many areas in the Lord's work that naturally attract us. However, this is truly damaging to us. When we see something naturally attractive in the Lord's work, we go about doing it! What a pity this is! For this reason, we must pray to God to grace us that we may know what it is to minister to God and to the house.

I have a very dear friend who is already on the other side of the veil. She belonged to the Lord, and I loved her very much in the Lord. One day the two of us were praying on a mountain, and afterward we read the portion of the Word in Ezekiel 44. She was much older than I, so she said, "Little brother, twenty years ago I read this portion of the Bible." I asked her how she had felt after reading it. She said, "When I came to this passage, I immediately closed the Bible, knelt down, and prayed, 'Lord, let me minister to You. Do not let me minister to the house.'" Brothers and sisters, I have not forgotten this incident, and I will never forget it. Although she has passed away, I remember her words all the time, "Lord, let me minister to You. Do not let me minister to the house." Can we pray such a prayer, saying, "Lord, I want to minister to You; I do not want to minister to the house"?

I fear very much that many lust for something of God yet do not want God Himself. Many think that saving souls is the most important thing, and they would give up their jobs to do this. The married sisters do not want to take care of the housework, the single sisters give up their consideration of marriage, and those who have a job do not want to work. They think that it is meaningless to continue doing what they are doing. They consider it irksome to work, take care of the family, serve, and study. They think that it would be wonderful if they could be released to preach the gospel. But friends, there are only two questions: Are you ministering to God? Or are you ministering to the house?

HOW TO MINISTER TO THE HOUSE AND HOW TO MINISTER TO THE LORD

Many like to exercise their muscles outside because by killing cattle and sheep, they can exercise their strength and fleshly energy. However, if you ask them to go to a quiet, solitary place where no one can see them, they are not able to do this. The sanctuary is an extremely dim place. Within there are only seven olive oil lamps which may not be as bright as seven candles! Many consider that ministering to the Lord in the sanctuary is not that interesting. But this is the place where the Lord wants us to be. Here it is calm and dark, and there are no crowds or great multitudes of people. Yet here one finds the genuine ministry to the Lord. Brothers, we cannot find a genuine servant of God or true minister to the Lord who does not minister in this way.

Now let us consider what the Levites were doing. They were killing cattle and sheep outside the house. Men can see you in such a place; the work is very apparent. Others will praise you, saying that you are wonderful and strong because you have killed many cattle and sheep and tied them to the altar. Many people are thrilled at the outward achievements of the work.

But what is involved in ministering to the Lord? Verse 15 says very clearly, "But the Levitical priests, the sons of Zadok, that kept the charge of My sanctuary when the children of Israel went astray from Me, they shall come near to Me to minister to Me; and they shall stand before Me to present to Me the fat and the blood, declares the Lord Jehovah." The basis for the ministry to the Lord, the basic requirement for ministering to the Lord, is to draw near to the Lord. It is to be bold enough to come before Him, to sit firmly before Him, and to stand before Him. Brothers, do we know how to draw near to the Lord? How often we find that we have to drag ourselves into His presence! Many indeed are fearful of being left alone in a dark room. They are afraid of being alone and cannot stand being shut in by themselves. Many times even though they are in a room, their heart is wandering outside, and they can no longer come near to the Lord. They cannot be alone by themselves and quietly learn to pray before Him. Many are very happy to work, join the crowd, and even preach to men. But how many can really draw near to God in the Holy of Holies? Many cannot draw near to God in that dim, quiet, and solitary sanctuary. However, no one can minister to Him without drawing near to Him. No one can minister to the Lord without approaching Him in prayer. Spiritual power is not the power of preaching but the power of praying. How much you pray indicates how much inner strength you really possess. No spiritual matter requires more strength than prayer. It is possible to read the Bible without exerting much effort. I am not saying that there is no effort involved in reading the Bible, but this is something that is rather easy to achieve. It is possible to preach the gospel without much effort, and it is possible to render help to the brothers without exerting much spiritual strength. In speaking, it is possible for one to rely on his memory to do the job. But in order to come to God and kneel before Him for an hour, there is the need for one to exert the strength of his whole being. Indeed, if one does not strive in such a way, he will not be able to maintain such a work; he will not be able to persevere. Every minister of the Lord knows the preciousness of such times: the sweetness of waking at midnight and spending an hour in prayer before going back to sleep, and the wonderful feeling of rising up very early in the morning for an hour's prayer. Unless we draw near to God, we cannot minister to Him. It is impossible to minister to the Lord and stand afar off at the same time. The disciples could follow the Lord from a far distance, but none of those who followed in that way could minister to Him. It is possible to follow the Lord secretly at a distance, but it is impossible to minister to Him in such a way. The sanctuary is the unique place where ministry to Him is possible. You can approach the people in the outer court, but you can approach God only in the sanctuary. Actually, those who can render help to the church and can do something are those who are near to God. If the labor before God is merely for the brothers and sisters, how poor the work will be.

If we want to minister to the Lord, we must draw near to Him. What should our condition be before God? "They shall stand before Me" (v. 15). It seems to me that we always want to be on the go, as if standing still were an impossible thing to do. We cannot stand still. Many brothers and sisters are extremely busy. There are many things before them, and they feel that they have to keep going. If you ask them to stand still and wait for awhile, they will not be able to do it. But all spiritual persons know what it is to stand before God.

What does it mean to stand? It means to wait for a command, to wait upon the Lord to speak His will. Countless numbers of works have been set up. I am not speaking of the work in factories and offices. Christians ought to be absolutely faithful to their earthly masters. We have to be very faithful in serving our earthly masters. But when it comes to spiritual work, we need to be more than just efficient. I speak in particular to all the co-workers. Brothers, is your work fully set? Is your work carried out efficiently? Can you not stand still and wait for awhile? Has much of your work been arranged and listed in order? Do you methodically work according to the list? Are you complete in everything? Brothers, can you wait for another three days? Can you stand still for a moment and not move around? This is to stand before the Lord. Everyone who does not know how to draw near to the Lord will surely not be able to minister to Him. Similarly, everyone who does not know how to stand before the Lord will surely not be able to minister to Him. It is impossible for them to minister to the Lord. Brothers, should not a servant wait for an order before he does anything?

Let me reiterate. Since this is a spiritual matter, I am not afraid of repetition. There are only two types of sin before God. One is rebellion against His command. If He gives an order and you refuse to do it, it is sin. But there is another type of sin, which is doing something without the Lord's command. One is the sin of rebellion, and the other is the sin of presumption. One ignores what the Lord has said; the other does what the Lord has not said. Standing before the Lord is the way to deal with the sin of doing what the Lord has not commanded. Brothers and sisters, how much of your spiritual work is done only after you are clear about God's will? How many really work as a result of the Lord's charge? Perhaps you work out of your zeal or because you consider it a good thing to do. Let me tell you that nothing damages God's will more than good things. Good things hinder God the most. We can easily recognize that as Christians we should not take part in evil, unclean, and lustful things and that these things are intolerable. Thus, it is unlikely for these things to be a hindrance to God's purpose. The things that hinder God's purpose are the good things, the things that are similar to His purpose. We may think that such a thing is not bad or that there is nothing better, and we may do it without asking if it is the Lord's will. Good things are God's greatest enemy. Indeed, every time we rebel against God, it is because we presume that something is good, and we go ahead and do it. As children of God, we all know that we cannot sin and that we should not do evil. But how often have we done something just because there was no conviction from the conscience or because the conscience thought it is all right to do?

No doubt, such a thing may be very good. But have we stood before the Lord? We need to stand before Him. Standing means to not walk or move; it means to remain in a place, to stand still and wait for the Lord's order. Brothers, this is the ministry to the Lord. The killing of cattle and sheep in the outer court is done whenever someone comes to offer a sacrifice. But in the Holy of Holies, there is utter solitude and no man in sight. In the Holy of Holies, no brother or sister has any authority over us, neither will a conference make decisions for us, nor does a committee have the authority to commission us. In the Holy of Holies, there is only one authority that will govern us, and that is the Lord. We will only do what the Lord directs us to do; otherwise, we will not do anything. Brothers, can we really stand before Him?

If we want to minister to the Lord in the Holy of Holies, we must spend time before the Lord and pray more. Otherwise, we will be inadequate. We need to pray to be ushered into God's presence and to draw near to Him. Hence, to pray is to stand before God; it is to seek His will before Him. Thank the Lord that although every believer does not do this, some are standing before the Lord and following Him in the journey ahead.

In order to stand before the Lord, it is necessary "to present to Me the fat and the blood" (Ezek. 44:15). We know that God is holy and righteous in the Holy Place and that God is glorious in the Holy of Holies. God's glory fills the Holy of Holies; God's holiness and righteousness fill the Holy Place. The blood is for God's holiness and righteousness, while the fat is for His glory. The fat is for God to gain something, while the blood deals with God's holiness and righteousness. We all know that God is holy and righteous and that He absolutely cannot accept anyone sinful. Without the shedding of blood or the remission of sin, without man paying a price for his sin, God will never be satisfied. Therefore, there is the need for the blood. There is no way to approach God without it. In the Old Testament time, man was put aside and could not come forward to God. But we can come before God because we have the Lord's blood. Not only so, but we also have to offer the fat, which means to offer the richest and best. We know that the blood deals with sin. But the fat is for God's satisfaction. The fat is the richest and best part, and it satisfies God's heart. Thus, it is for God's glory.

All those who would come before God to minister to Him must answer to God's holiness, righteousness, and even His glory. The entire Bible, both the Old Testament and the New Testament, focuses on these three things: God's holiness, God's righteousness, and God's glory. God's glory refers to God Himself; God's holiness refers to His nature; and God's righteousness refers to His way. In other words, God's way is righteous, God's nature is holy, and God Himself is glory. Every time we come before God, we must first realize how we are able to stand before God. God is holy and righteous! How can sinners like us meet Him? We can meet Him because the blood is here, remitting and cleansing us from our sin. As a result, we can approach God without any conflict because

His blood has cleansed us from all unrighteousness. However, He is not only holy and righteous; He is also glorious in Himself. Therefore, there is a need to offer the fat, which is to offer up our very best to God for His satisfaction. In other words, the blood deals with everything in the old creation, and the fat speaks of everything in the new creation. The blood dispels everything of the old creation, so that we no longer have a problem concerning holiness and righteousness. The fat is of the new creation, which signifies the offering of ourselves to God, so that we no longer have a problem with God's glory.

We cannot minister to God if we do not know death and resurrection. Death is not a doctrine or a theory from the Bible; it is poured out through a genuine trust in Him and in the pouring out of His incorruptible blood. When His incorruptible blood was poured out, we too were poured out. Thank the Lord. Now our Lord has no blood. He only has a body with bones and flesh. Everything of the natural life was poured out. When the Lord's blood was poured out, everything of the soul-life was poured out. He indeed poured out His soul unto death (Isa. 53:12). This is the significance of the blood. The pouring out of the blood is the removal of everything natural. (We will speak more concerning this matter later.)

If we want to minister before God, we need to draw near to Him, stand before Him, and wait for His will. Please remember these two indispensable matters. On the one hand, we must continually pour out "our blood"—we must continually acknowledge that everything we have by birth and lose by death has been poured out. Many frequently ask me what the natural life really is. I often answer them by saying that everything that comes with birth and goes with death is of the natural life; everything that exists between birth and death is the natural life. Praise the Lord! He has already poured out everything of our natural life. In other words, He has poured out everything that we obtained and everything that came by birth. When the Lord poured out His blood, He did not only pour out His own life, but ours as well. Hence, we have to continually stand on this fact and deny our soul-life. Brothers and sisters, this is altogether not a doctrine but a reality. Everything of the natural life is thus dropped before God. Brothers and sisters, this is a goal that we can attain to because, in Christ, everything of the soul has been poured out so that it is now possible for us to be selfless. Thank the Lord, we can be selfless because Christ poured out our self when He poured out His blood. By ourselves, this is impossible; we cannot crucify ourselves. Thank the Lord that the Son of God has accomplished this fact. By Him we can die, and by Him we can give up our self. But it is not sufficient just to die, because death is only the negative side. Our focus before God is not only on death but also on resurrection. When He arose, we were in Him. In Him, we became a new creation. He not only died but also rose from the dead. He lives unto God; therefore, all that He is, is for God's satisfaction and not for Himself. Brothers and sisters, this is what God wants to show us. This is what it is to minister to the Lord. We must offer Him the fat and the blood.

Verse 16 says, "It is they who will enter My sanctuary, and it is they who will come near to My table to minister to Me, and they will keep My charge." This verse tells us that there is a place to minister to the Lord. The ministry to the Lord is in the sanctuary—a hidden, quiet place not public like the outer court. Brothers and sisters, may He grace us so that we would not consider it a suffering to be in the sanctuary. Actually, a day there is better than a thousand days in another place. Yet we are always afraid of the sanctuary. How good it is to be in the outer court! Everyone can see us there. How good it is to be in the outer court! They all know us there. How good it is to be in the outer court! Our names are well known, and there is no attack or slander there, only a welcome and praises. How wonderful this is! But God wants us to be in the sanctuary. When we are in that place, others may say that we are lazy and not doing anything. In reality, what is done there is far superior to the work of ministering to the people in the outer court. Have you heard others criticizing you for being small and narrow? Have you heard others say that you will not do this or that? Others may say that you are too lazy to work and that you have left many things undone. But brothers and sisters, our hearts are not narrow at all. We are not asking anything of men, and we do not want to stand at the gate for many to see. We have only one goal, which is to minister to the Lord in the Holy Place. Brothers and sisters, we are not willing to minister in the house because our hope and our task are greater than this. No one here is as ambitious as Paul was. He had one ambition, which was to please the Lord. The things we are seeking here are greater than many other things, and our labor here is greater than that of many who do great works. The fact is that our heart is broader than anyone else's. Brothers, do not think that we are too small and narrow. We are very broad, for we are not only ministering to the house but to the Lord as well. Of course this is not that great in the sight of man. Brothers and sisters, we would rather let others criticize us than to move without God's will. We have only two positions here: one is that we are dead and have dropped everything of the old creation; the other is that we are resurrected and are serving God, learning to stand before Him, listening to His order, and waiting in His presence to minister to Him. We do not care for anything else. O brothers and sisters, is God's will enough to satisfy you? Is it enough to do His will? Is His will good enough? Or are you still pursuing other things? Are all of God's plans for you good enough? Oh, you must learn to minister to God in His presence.

Since time is so short and we also have to cover Luke 17, I cannot share in more detail. I have said earlier that I wanted to mention three things. One is the difference between ministering to the house and ministering to the Lord; another is the way to minister to the house and the way to minister to the Lord; and the third is the requirements and condition of one who ministers to the Lord. Now let us consider the requirements of one who ministers to the Lord.

THE REQUIREMENTS OF ONE WHO MINISTERS TO THE LORD

Those who ministered to God before Him had to be clothed with linen garments, linen bonnets on their heads, and linen breeches on their loins. Their whole body was clothed with linen material. Verse 17 also says that no wool should come upon them. No one who ministered to the Lord could be clothed with wool. Before God, no one could ever put on woolen garments. Why? Please read Ezekiel 44:18: "They shall have linen turbans on their heads and have linen trousers over their loins; they shall not gird themselves with anything that causes sweat." This portion of the Word reveals that all those who minister to the Lord should not sweat. All work that produces sweat is not pleasing to God and is rejected by Him. What is the meaning of sweat? The first sweat in the entire world was shed by Adam when he was driven out of the garden of Eden. Genesis 3 tells us that, due to Adam's sin, God punished him by saying, "By the sweat of your face / You will eat bread." Sweat is a result of the curse. Due to God's curse, the ground ceased to yield its fruit; due to the absence of God's blessing, human effort is necessary, and this causes sweat. What is the work that causes sweat? It is the work that comes out of human effort without the blessing from God the Father. Everyone ministering to God should absolutely abstain from any work that causes sweat. Numerous works placed before God require effort and running around for their accomplishment. Everyone ministering to God must do a work that causes no sweat. All of God's work is serene; it is not accomplished by running around but by sitting down. Although outwardly one may be very busy, he is very restful within; although outwardly it is hot, within it is very calm. This work is done by sitting down. This is the work that causes no sweat! All the real work before God is not accidental and not accomplished by fleshly effort. Unfortunately, so much of today's work cannot be accomplished without sweating. What a pity that today's work cannot be accomplished unless someone is planning, sponsoring, promoting, proposing, running around, admonishing, exhorting, and exerting human effort and fleshly strength. Oh, it is really a pity that in most cases, without sweat, there is no work. Please bear in mind that sweating outside is permissible. In slaying cattle and sheep outside, serving sinners, and ministering to the saints, sweating is permissible. If you are doing that kind of work, you can sweat all you want. But those who minister to the Lord in the Holy Place absolutely cannot sweat. God does not need man's sweating. No doubt, all work is busy, but God's work does not need fleshly strength. I do not mean that there is no need of spiritual strength. In fact, how much spiritual strength you need and how much suffering you have to go through is hard to say. No one cares to distinguish between spiritual work and fleshly work. Men conclude that all of God's work cannot be accomplished without running around, spending time to discuss and debate, negotiating, proposing, approving, and authorizing. Yet if you ask them to wait quietly before God and listen to His speaking, they cannot do it because the flesh is not capable of doing this. Oh, all these require sweating.

The most important aspect of spiritual work is to deal with God. The first person we should contact is God, not man. The work of the flesh is different; the first one it contacts is man. Hence, if a work cannot be accomplished without man, it is not the work of God. How precious it is to be in God's presence. We have to deal with Him alone. We are not idle; rather, we are doing a work that causes no sweat. What does this mean? If we deal properly with God, there is no need to sweat before man. We can accomplish the most amount of work with the least amount of strength. The reason there are so many advertisements, promotions, and proposals is because men are not praying before God. Let me say that all spiritual work is done only before God. If we take care of our work properly before God, we will not need many ways. Others will spontaneously respond to us and spontaneously profit. God is working, and there is no need of human strength and sweating.

Brothers and sisters, we should examine ourselves very honestly before God. Let us ask Him, "O Lord, am I really ministering to You or to the work? O Lord, is my ministry unto the house or unto You?" If we are sweating from morning till evening, then we can surely say to ourselves that we are ministering to the house and not to the Lord. If all our business and laboring are to meet outward needs, we can conclude that we are ministering to people and not to God. I do not despise such people, for they also are doing God's work. There is a need for some to slay the cattle and sheep. There is a need for some to lead and guide others. The children of Israel needed some to minister to them. But God desires something much deeper. We ought to pray to Him, "O God! I beg You to deliver me that I might not fall into the realm of ministering to the people." There is more than just ministering to the people. Brothers and sisters, too many are already ministering to the people. Why do we still want to add our portion there? God has no way to demand everyone to minister to Him; God cannot do this since many are not willing to minister to Him. Because man is not willing, it is impossible to revive the whole church and cause everyone to become faithful. Many are truly saved and have God's life, yet they just want to minister to the people. There is no way to change them because they do not want to miss the excitement on the outside. They will not let go of the work on the outside; their focus is on the field of work. Surely, there are some who need to take care of these matters. But the question is, are we among those taking part in these things? I hope we all can say to the Lord, "O God, I want to minister to You. I am willing to drop everything, to let go of all the work and forsake all the outward things. I want to minister to You and do a spiritual work. I am willing to give up all the outward things. I want to enter within, more deeply within."

There was no way for God to ask all the Levites to come. He could only choose the sons of Zadok. Why? Because when the children of Israel turned against the ways of the Lord and forsook Him, the sons of Zadok kept the charge of the sanctuary. They saw that what was on the outside was beyond repair; what was on the outside had collapsed and was contaminated. So they left what was on the outside and concentrated on keeping the sanctuary holy. Brothers and sisters, can you let what is on the outside collapse? Perhaps you will use wood to support it, so that the structure will not collapse. But the Lord will say, "I do not care for these things. I will only preserve My sanctuary and reserve a place that is holy for My children." There is the need of a place to be wholly separated and sanctified to Him; a place where one can discern between what is proper and what is improper. God wants to preserve His sanctuary. What is on the outside is collapsing, and God has no way but to let it go. Since the sons of Zadok did what they did, God chose them. Truly, God has no way to deal with everyone, but He wants to deal with you! If you are not willing to let go of everything on the outside, to whom can God go? Brothers and sisters, I stand in the presence of God to beg you all; God is seeking those who will fully minister to Him. There are really too many who are working on the outside. Those who are ministering to God on the inside are far too few. This is why God is crying, "Who will minister to Me in My sanctuary?"

Oh! I cannot say too much about this matter. I can only say that I very much enjoy reading Acts 13: "Now there were in Antioch, in the local church, prophets and teachers....And as they were ministering to the Lord and fasting, the Holy Spirit said, Set apart for Me now Barnabas and Saul for the work to which I have called them" (vv. 1-2). Such is the work of the New Testament. It is also the unique principle for the work of the New Testament. The work of the Holy Spirit can only be revealed at the time of ministering to the Lord. Only at the time of ministering to the Lord will the Holy Spirit send some forth. If we do not place ministering to the Lord as the top priority, everything will be out of order.

The work of the church in Antioch began during the time of ministering to the Lord. The Holy Spirit said, "Set apart for Me now Barnabas and Saul for the work to which I have called them." I repeat again, God does not want men to volunteer for His army. The soldiers who volunteer for the army are not wanted by God. God only has conscripted, or drafted, soldiers. We know that there are two kinds of soldiers in an army: one kind volunteer to join the army, and the other kind are drafted by the country. Based on the orders of the country, they have no choice except to serve as soldiers. But in the Lord's work, there are only drafted soldiers; there are no voluntary soldiers. Therefore, no one can say, because of his preference, he will go and preach the gospel; God will not use him. God's work has been greatly damaged by too many volunteer soldiers. They cannot declare as the Lord has declared, "Him who sent Me..." O brothers and sisters, this is not a light matter. God's work cannot be accomplished according to our will. God's work is completely His. We must check to see if this work is out of ourselves or out of the Lord's call. We must ask ourselves if we have volunteered to join the army or if we have been drafted by God. All the volunteer soldiers will not last; all those who recommended themselves will not last because God only wants soldiers who have been drafted by Him. When they ministered to the Lord, Paul and Barnabas did not say, "We will go forth to spread the gospel." Rather, the Holy Spirit said, "*Set apart for Me* now Barnabas and Saul for the work to which *I have called* them." Only the Holy Spirit has the authority to commission men to work. Concerning this matter, the church has no authority at all. Yet within many missionary societies and crusades there is the sending forth of men by men. God never allows such things. We should only minister to the Lord, not to the house. God desires to have those who will minister to Him directly and receive the commission by the Holy Spirit directly.

I say again, to minister to the Lord is not to forsake all the work on the outside. To minister to the Lord is not to give up serving in the villages. What I say is that all the work on the outside should be based on our ministry to the Lord. We go forth, out from our ministry to the Lord, rather than out from our own desires, which have no basis in the ministry to the Lord. There is a vast difference between these two matters. The difference is greater than that between heaven and earth. All those with experience realize that there is no difference greater than the difference between ministering to the Lord and ministering to the house.

It is one thing to know about the veil; we should minister to the Lord in the sanctuary. But beyond the veil, there is another matter which is just as important: "Let us therefore go forth unto Him outside the camp, bearing His reproach" (Heb. 13:13). The central thought of the book of Hebrews comprises these two things: the veil and the camp. Not only do we need to minister to God in the sanctuary, but we also need to go outside the camp. It is only when we have left the camp to minister to the Lord that He will speak and lead; at other times, He will not speak.

Let us now take a look at what Luke says. Let us clarify this once again: we do not want to expound on Luke. Rather, we want to find out from this portion of the Word what the Lord really wants. Luke 17:7-10 tells us very clearly that the Lord is satisfied with nothing other than Himself. He does not want you and me; He wants Himself. It is amazing that although the words here are quite severe, everyone feels that this portion is precious. There are two kinds of work here: one is plowing, or we may say, sowing. The other is the shepherding, or we may say, feeding. The work of sowing deals with those not yet regenerated. The work of shepherding deals with those who possess the life of God. Consequently, one kind of work concerns sinners, and the other kind of work concerns believers. These works cause those who have not received the Lord to receive the Lord and those who have received the Lord to be fed. Such is the work of the Lord's servants. This is also what we should do in the presence of God. This work is vital, and we must do our best. But the Lord is very amazing here. He said, "But which of you, having a slave who is plowing or tending sheep, will say to him when he has come in from the field, Come immediately and recline at table?" (Luke 17:7). This means that He would not do it this way. In other words, the servants, the Christians, should not be given food to eat after their work is done. Fleshly ones will say, "What a harsh Employer! We are extremely tired from plowing and feeding the cattle outside. Now that we are home, You should serve us food." But the Lord is not like a worldly master. (A different relationship between the earthly master and the servant is mentioned in Colossians and Ephesians. What is spoken of here is the treatment the Lord expects toward Himself. This is about the relationship between the spiritual master and the servant.) The Lord does not invite us to eat. What does He want then? Verse 8 says, "Will he not rather say to him"—that is, surely he will say to him—"Prepare something that I may dine, and gird yourself and serve me." This is what the Lord is doing. We always think to ourselves, "Today I have plowed so many acres of land and sown so many pounds of seeds. After so many days, so many months, there will be at least a thirty or sixty-fold harvest. Today I led so many sheep to the green pastures, to a certain spot in a certain place, and they drank beside the still waters. After so much time, these sheep will surely grow big and fat. This is indeed the greatest work. The produce from the land may serve as food; the products from the flock of sheep may serve as clothing." We are glad and enjoy the happiness from our labor. The meaning of eating and drinking is the enjoyment that comes out of our recollection of the work we have done. How often, after we have made some proud achievements, do we think about them even while we are sleeping and relish them in our memory. We may even think about them while we are eating and feel very proud and satisfied. Often we call to mind something and are thrilled by such thoughts. But the Lord said His goal for all the work, whether it be feeding the cattle or plowing the field, is not to make us happy, give us enjoyment, or let us have some gain. The Lord will surely say to us, "Prepare something that I may dine, and gird yourself and serve Me." Do we see this? What the Lord demands is that we minister to Him. Please remember that the work in the fields cannot be compared to the work at home. Please remember that the land and the cattle cannot be compared to the Lord. The Lord does not say here, "Since you labored so hard, plowed so much land, and fed so many cattle, you need not serve Me anymore; you may go to eat, drink and be merry." The Lord's words inform us how He weighs the importance of our labor and our need to minister to Him. He will not let us go just because we have plowed the land, fed the cattle, and done so much work on the outside; He will not tell us that there is no need to minister to Him. The Lord will not do this. He will by no means do this. He will not allow us to omit the ministering to Him just because we are too occupied with our work. He will not allow the hardship of the labor to rob Him of our ministry to Him. The first priority is to minister to the

Lord because ministering to the Lord is more vital than all the plowing, feeding, and working.

Brothers and sisters, what are we really doing? What is our goal? Do we only care for plowing and sowing? Do we only care for preaching the gospel to save sinners? Do we only care for shepherding and feeding cattle? Do we only care to dispense food for the edification of the believers? Or are we satisfying the Lord with food and drink? The Lord is showing us here that after we come home we should not rest and be slothful. Although we are tired, we still need to endeavor to serve Him. Although we have worked much and suffered much, this cannot take the place of the ministering that He should receive. We need to forget all our experience and serve Him once again. But this is not to say that we do not need to eat. It merely means that our eating and drinking should come after the Lord's. We should also be filled and satisfied. Yet this should be after the Lord is filled and satisfied. We should also be happy. Yet this should be after the Lord's happiness. Therefore, let us ask ourselves to whom the glory of the work goes. Is everything that we are doing really for the satisfaction of the Lord's heart? Or is it for the satisfaction of our heart? Is the fruit of the labor for the Lord's satisfaction? Or is it for our own satisfaction? I deeply fear that many times the Lord has not gained anything, and yet we are satisfied. I deeply fear that many times before the Lord is happy, we are already very happy. We need to ask God to show us where we should stand in His presence and how we should really minister to Him in His presence.

Brothers and sisters, even if we do everything, we are nothing but useless servants. We are indeed very small.

Our goal and our striving are not the land and cattle, the world and the church. Our goal is the Lord. We are also striving for the Lord. He is our everything. Therefore, let us ask ourselves: Is the work we do truly for Christ, or is it only for sinners and brothers? Whoever can discern the difference between the ministry to sinners and the ministry to the Lord, and whoever can discern the difference between the ministry to the brothers and the ministry to the Lord, is blessed. In theory it seems easy to make such a distinction; yet to be able to inwardly distinguish the difference in our experience is a blessing. This kind of knowledge does not come easily. It requires the shedding of blood before the lesson can be learned. This kind of discernment is not easily apprehended. It requires many dealings before we can know it. Many times it requires the putting down of our life and the killing of our opinions before we can truly comprehend it. Ministering to the Lord is not as easy as ministering to the brothers and the sisters. Therefore, there is a vast difference between ministering to the Lord and ministering to the house.

Nevertheless, if the Holy Spirit works in us, it will not be that difficult for us to know. We need to ask the Lord to grant us grace, revelation, and light, so that we may see what ministering to Him means. A ministry to the sinners and a ministry to the Lord are two entirely different things; ministering to sinners is altogether different from ministering to the Lord. Brothers and sisters, sinners are not more important than the Lord. We need to ask the Lord to work on us, so that we will minister to Him. I cannot say anything more. I can only say that this is what the Lord wants to speak to us in these few days. ❧

5

HAVING BEEN MADE DEAD TO THE LAW

"So then, my brothers,
you also have been made dead to the law
through the body of Christ so that you might be
joined to another, to Him who has been raised from the dead,
that we might bear fruit to God."
Romans 7:4

Scripture Reading:
Romans 7:4, 15-19

Romans 7 is a very familiar chapter to us. Not only is it familiar to us in our reading, it is also familiar to us in our experience. We often read Romans 7 and often practice Romans 7. What the Lord wants me to speak on today is the way to be delivered from the demand of the law, that is, the way to be delivered from ourselves.

WHO CAN RECEIVE GOD'S DELIVERANCE

Before we speak on the subject of deliverance and the way to be delivered, I will first mention one qualification. What type of persons are qualified to speak about deliverance? Brothers and sisters, although God's deliverance is for everyone, not everyone receives deliverance. Although it is possible for everyone to be delivered from the law, not everyone is actually delivered. The problem is absolutely not with God but with man, because man does not want to be delivered and has not paid the price for deliverance. The apostle who wrote Romans 7 was eventually delivered because he paid the price; he hated something and he willed to do something. The biggest problem that confronts us today is that we are not yet delivered. Yet I would like to ask if we have deeply hated the temper that we have not been able to overcome. Have we deeply hated the sin that causes us to fall and the things that stumble us all the time? Or are we willing to say that sinning is something common to all Christians and is, therefore, unavoidable? Do we sense a hatred for the unclean thoughts, the sinful deeds, the entangling temper, and the evil lusts; do we look for deliverance from them? The apostle not only speaks of deliverance in this chapter but also of his feeling before his deliverance. Before he was delivered, he hated what he repeatedly did. He did not practice what he willed, and he did what he hated. The first question is whether we love or hate the things that we are doing. The apostle experienced deliverance because he deeply hated and desperately sought for deliverance. He was so disgusted with his life of sin that he could no longer tolerate it; he felt that he could no longer go along with it. He hated it so much that he wished to die. He would not allow it to go on for a moment longer. He experienced the deliverance because he had such a determination.

Brothers and sisters, do you have such a hunger within? Have you ever said that you cannot continue to live a life that is bound and entangled with sin? Have you realized how loathsome such a living is? Brothers and sisters, the words which God commissioned me to speak this morning are only for those who desire deliverance and consider that the level of their Christian life is too low. My words are not for those who are self-satisfied and content with living in sin and failure. They are for those who seek deliverance and have not found the way. They are not for those who think it is all right to lose one's temper, to be lustful, or have unclean thoughts. Neither are they for those who think that they only need to confess when they have failed and that everything will be all right as soon as God forgives their sins. The victory in Romans 7 is for those who experience the failures like those in Romans 7. Anyone who is not saved cannot experience this kind of deliverance. Only those who hate their present living and do not wish to continue with such a living can experience this victory. Those who live in failure and sin, not realizing that they have to reject these things, will never find God's deliverance coming to them.

Every time a person wants to have spiritual growth in his life before God, he must first be dissatisfied with his present living. All growth begins from dissatisfaction. One must be pressed to such an extent that he feels he cannot go on anymore, that he has reached the end of himself, and that his living is unacceptable. He must consider that it is no longer acceptable to be bound by the self, the world, and sin; and it is no longer acceptable that what he wills, he does not do, and what he hates, he does. He has to recognize that such a contradictory life cannot go on and that there must be a way out. God will grant His deliverance only to those who are living under these conditions. Therefore, we have a great need before God to ask Him to give us the grace to not be content with our life of sin and failure. Every victory begins with a realization of our failure and wickedness. Everyone who desires deliverance must first be so pressed that he feels he cannot go on. Only then can he experience deliverance. I am merely telling the way; actual deliverance can only come from God. In other words, while I am giving the light, only God gives the revelation directly. Light cannot save; only revelation can save.

THE MEANING OF BEING DELIVERED FROM THE LAW

Romans 7 is a great chapter, and we cannot cover all of it today. We will only mention verse 4. In this verse, the first thing mentioned is: "So then, my brothers, you also have been made dead to the law." In other words, we are dead to the law. Brothers, have we realized that we need to be delivered from the law? If I say that we should be delivered from sin, everybody understands because sin is loathsome, and it is right to be delivered from it. If I say that we should be delivered from the world, everyone also understands because the world has crucified our Lord and is indeed evil. If I say that we should be delivered from ourselves, everyone also understands because the flesh is something evil. If I say that we should be delivered from uncleanness or licentiousness, we can still understand. But if I say that we should be delivered from the law, some may say that they do not feel the need for such a deliverance. If the apostle says that we need to be delivered from the self, we say, "Amen." If he says that we need to be delivered from the world or sin, we would again say, "Amen." But when he says that we have been delivered from the law or that we are dead to the law, we do not know how to respond. We realize that what the apostle said cannot be wrong, but we do not understand why he said it. We understand deliverance from sin, from the self, and from the world. But we cannot understand the reason for deliverance from the law. Why did the apostle tell us that we are delivered from the law and that we are dead to the law? What does deliverance have to do with the law? It has a great deal to do with it. Deliverance from the law has a great deal to do with deliverance from the world, from sin, and from the self. Therefore, this is a very important matter.

Brothers and sisters, if we desire to experience deliverance, it is very important that we realize that God has no more hope in us. If we are seeking deliverance, we first need to understand ourselves and realize that we are hopeless. We have to clearly see how God evaluates us and how we evaluate ourselves. All of us belong to Christ; we are His. We may have been Christians for many years, but I am afraid that we have lived a life of failures and frequent stumblings and downfalls. But what happens after each failure? Almost everyone makes a resolution after a failure, saying to himself, "Next time I will do better and will not fail." Every failure brings another heartache and self-condemnation, and the question is raised once more, "Why did I do this? Why did I fail again? I am a believer and should not be this way. This is too poor!" You become very disheartened. After you fail, as with almost everyone, there are two results. First, you resolve to do better the next time. Second, you feel sorry and sigh, looking back at what you have done and asking why you are so bad. This is what you do all the time. When you fail, you are heartbroken and ask, "How could I have fallen so low? I will never do anything like that again. Lord, deliver me from this!" Your experience is similar to that of Romans 7. Before one heartache goes away, another occasion for heartache comes. One resolution has not worked, but you still find yourself making a second resolution. This goes on time after time and things still do not improve. This is your situation. What is the reason for this? The reason is that you have not yet been delivered from the law, and have not yet seen what the law is, and what being delivered from the law is.

If you want to understand what it is to be delivered from the law, you must first understand the relationship that the law has with us. The law is God's requirement on our flesh. The law is God telling us that we should or should not do something. It is what God says concerning what we ought and ought not to do. It is what God forbids or commands us to do. Therefore, the law is God's requirement on us. In brief, the law is all the demands that God places on those who are in Adam and all the commands that God gives to those who are in Adam, commands that tell them what they should or should not do. (God does this to prove the corruption and the hopelessness of the flesh.) Not only can God put us under the law, but we, who are in Adam, can also put ourselves under the law, hoping that we can please God. We set up ordinances for ourselves to keep, saying, "I should not do this. I should not do that." In addition to the commandments that God has given us, we have also given ourselves many other commandments which are just as severe as the ones God has given. Therefore, God puts His demands on us, and we also put demands on ourselves. This means that we still have a hope in the things of Adam, thinking that we can improve and striving to advance and overcome. Brothers and sisters, God has put us under the law, and at the same time we have put ourselves under the law.

What does it mean to be delivered from the law? It is to entirely lose hope in ourselves. Not only should we entirely lose hope in ourselves, but we should not hope at all. Do not hope for anything concerning ourselves any longer. This is the way to be delivered from the law. God allows us to sin day after day in order to make us realize that we are corrupt and unclean, and it is impossible to improve. We cannot overcome, and we cannot keep the law. There is no possibility for us to be helped; we are completely useless, and we are not improving. God wants us to realize that the reason He crucified us on the cross, which He did in Christ, is because we are corrupt beyond any hope. When we consider ourselves to be hopeless and realize that God considers us to be hopeless, we will only stand on the position God gives us. God says that we are corrupt to the core and hopeless. We need to say the same thing, that we are corrupt to the core and hopeless. All that we can do is sin. We do not cherish any hope about ourselves anymore. This is what it is to be delivered from the law. What a great deliverance this is! *The unique way of deliverance is to consider ourselves as being hopeless.*

The last time I was in Canada, I met a certain Mr. G. He was a good man and was also good in the gospel. God used him to save many sinners. Now he is old, over sixty years of age. One day we were walking on the street and talking, and we came to this topic. He said that this is the lesson we have to preach to others all the time. I asked him what he meant, and he began to tell me his history: "When I was a young believer, I was very zealous. I wanted to serve the Lord well, advance, and make myself good. But things always turned out the opposite way. The more I tried, the worse I became, and the more I realized that I could not make it. I was disappointed as well as bewildered. I found no solution. One day another brother said to me, 'Mr. G., God never cherishes the hope that you cherish for yourself. You have so much hope for yourself, but God has no hope in you!' I was very surprised and asked him what God had to say about me. He said, 'God knows that you are powerless and that you cannot do anything. You are hopeless. *This is why* He crucified you on the cross. What you deserve is only crucifixion and nothing else.' From that day on, the scales seemed to fall from my eyes. I saw that God has not required anything of me, and I saw that I could do nothing. *This is why* He crucified me on the cross. If that is the case, why do I still need to struggle?"

Brothers and sisters, in theory and in doctrine we know very well that the old Adamic life is irreparable and incurable. But the surprising thing is that in our experience, we still try to repair and improve it; we still cherish hope for the Adamic life. Many people say, "I am surprised that I still commit such a sin!" But I say that we should be surprised if we no longer committed such a sin! Is there any sin that we could not commit? We can commit any sin; the root of all sins is in us. God considers us hopeless and impossible to reform. This is why He crucified us on the cross. When the Lord died, we died also. God's crucifixion of us on the cross is His evaluation of us. In effect, God is saying that we deserve only death and annihilation.

Brothers and sisters, how different is our evaluation of ourselves from God's evaluation of us. We think that we are able to do something. We think that we can overcome, be holy, and make progress. But God does not cherish any such hope. All we are from head to toe is sin; we are absolutely useless. There is no way to save us except by the way of death. Without death, there can be no deliverance. We always think that there is still a chance for improvement and victory. But there is no such thing. Today we see the first fact, which is God's evaluation of us, how much He thinks we are worth. Brothers and sisters, the ones who see this are blessed before others. Countless numbers of Christians have experienced repeated stumblings, defilements, failures, disappointments, and journeys of hopelessness before they see that God has *absolutely no hope* in them. The sooner we see this fact, the better it will be for us, because this is the starting point of all deliverance. All genuine release of life begins here. We should see that we deserve nothing but death. The sooner we see this, the faster we will grow. The whole problem hinges on how we view the old Adamic life. We know and have mentioned this over a hundred times: the old Adamic life is irreparable and unalterable. But how many of us have *really seen* that we deserve to die? How many have seen that there is not another way besides death? Understanding the doctrine is one thing, knowing and seeing is another. Doctrines can only make us understand something in the mind, but seeing requires revelation in our spirit. All the things which do not come from God's revelation and from our seeing are the things that do not count; they are not effective at all.

The meaning of being delivered from the law is to be delivered from God's demands. This means that we have ceased all hope of pleasing God; this comes as a result of understanding the Adamic life and the work of Christ. We no longer hope to do anything to please God. As long as we still hope to please God by our own effort, we are not yet delivered from the law, and we will not be able to avoid heartaches and disappointments. The only way not to be disappointed is for us to know that God has no more hope in us.

HOW TO BE DELIVERED FROM THE LAW

We have seen that, first, we need to be delivered from the law. But how can we be delivered from the law? The only way is death. Death can deliver us from the law because as long as we live, the law will have a demand on us. A living person is not supposed to break the law because the law will punish him. This is what the apostle said, that as long as the husband lives, the law puts its demands on the wife. However, if he dies, the power of the law will not reach her and will not make demands on her. Therefore, to be delivered from the demand of the law, there is no way except by death. As long as we live, the law will continue to put its demand on us.

For now, I will not speak of how God's law puts its demand on us; I will only speak of how we make demands on ourselves by our own enacted law. When do we do this? If we get up late today, we resolve to get up early tomorrow. We make resolutions to overcome when we are very defiled, when we struggle day and night with sin, when we are in the turbulent current of the world, and when we feel that our life is very wrong. We think that we can make it, that we are able to make it, and that we will make it. In this way, we consider ourselves still to be alive. But by doing this, we will not see the clear work of Christ in us. If we truly know God, we will realize that He has completely given up hope in us. This is why He had no other option than to crucify us on the cross. If we really see that we are only worthy of death, all our resolutions will be gone. I can speak the same thing for myself. Many times I resolved that I would never do such and such a thing again. But afterward, I asked myself again, "Are you not worthy of death? If you are, why do you still make resolutions?" Therefore, we must see that the way to overcome is not by making resolutions but by standing on the ground where God has placed us. We should not cherish the hope that the next time will be better. Instead, we only stand on the ground where God has put us. We should not make resolutions anymore, nor should we hope to advance. We should no longer struggle to overcome because we know that all these are the works of the old Adamic life. We have to put them in the place of death and ignore them. If we are truly standing in the place of death, we will overcome and experience deliverance from all these things. Therefore, death is our only way; it is the unique way of salvation. The world, sin, the self—nothing is able to touch a dead person. If we consider all these things as dead, they will not touch us anymore.

HAVING DIED IN CHRIST

Now we will go one step further to consider how we have died. Verse 4 says, "So then, my brothers, you also have been made dead to the law through the body of Christ." From this we see that our death is "through the body of Christ." In the same way that Christ died, we died. The time that Christ died is the time that we died. Christ has died, and we have died too. This is not a spiritual suicide, in which we artificially consider ourselves to be dead. Nor is it a repeated declaration to ourselves that we are dead, in an effort to signal to ourselves that we are dead. Rather, when we see Christ's accomplished fact on the cross and realize that God has included us in this death of Christ, we are led to the inevitable conclusion that we have died. There are two spiritual experiences in this world which are most amazing. The first is seeing God's plan, that is, what God has planned for us and what God thinks we should do.

For example, He has judged that we are dead. The second is to see what God has done in Christ for us. These two things are very wonderful. We see what God has ordained for us, we see how we have become one with Christ, and we see how, in Him, we can receive all that He has accomplished. When Jesus Christ was crucified on the cross, we were included in His death because God has included us in Him. When His body was broken, we were broken as well. His crucifixion is our crucifixion. Therefore, we and Christ are one. This is why we pay attention to the matter of baptism. Many people say that baptism is only an outward ritual and not important. No, it is altogether a testimony of something inward. We believe that when Christ died, we also died. The first thing after a death is burial and this is why we bury ourselves in the water of baptism. If we do not believe that we are dead, we would not be buried. The fact that we are willing to be buried means that we believe we are dead. Therefore, baptism is to believe that Christ has died and that we also have died. This is why we bury ourselves. The burial is a proof that we are dead. Christ has been crucified. When He was crucified on the cross, we were included in Him. When the veil was rent, the cherubim were rent as well. The veil was rent from top to bottom; it was God who rent it from top to bottom. At the same time, the cherubim were also rent by God from top to bottom because the cherubim were sewn on the veil. We know that the veil is the body of Christ, while the cherubim are God's creatures. Therefore, when Christ died, all of God's creation died. This is what it means to be dead to the law through the body of Christ.

The way of deliverance is not to deliberately reckon ourselves dead. Those who have been preaching the doctrine of reckoning themselves dead are preaching the wrong teaching. What is the right teaching? The right teaching is to reckon ourselves dead *in Christ*. We do not die in ourselves; rather, we die through *the body of Christ*. Christ died, and since we are joined to Him, we also died. The secret to victory is *never to look at ourselves apart from Christ and never to consider the self that is outside of Christ*. This is what the Lord meant in John 15 when He said that we should abide in

Him. It means that we should never look at ourselves apart from Christ. What is outside is still very uncomely and cannot be improved. If we want to look at ourselves, we can only look at ourselves in Christ. Once we look at the self outside of Christ, we will immediately fail. Many times we forget the facts that Christ has accomplished. We become angry and frustrated at ourselves and ask why we are the way we are. We continue to fail, fall, and suffer disappointment with a resulting loss of heart. Please remember that these are the things that a person does outside of Christ. Today, in Christ, I have died to the law. If anyone has not received this deliverance and freedom, I would invite you to look at yourself only in Christ. In Christ, God has crucified us because He has judged us irreparable. There is no way to save us except by death. Therefore, God has judged us to be dead, and He has crucified us together in Christ. We are therefore free and delivered from the demands of the law. There are two facts here which we have to absolutely stand on. The first is that God has considered us absolutely hopeless. Only death can deliver us from the law. The second is that in Christ God has crucified us on the cross. The first has to do with God's plan, while the second has to do with God's work. The first is what God has destined, while the second is what God has accomplished. God knows that there is no other way of salvation except through death. We have been broken into pieces, and there is no way for us to become whole again. Herein lies the basis of our redemption—the cross. For this reason, in our daily life we should accept this fact all the time so that we can be delivered from the law. If we stand on this ground, we will not find obstructions. Of course, we should confess and ask God for forgiveness when we fail. But we do not need to look back, because all the failures and degradations come from the old Adamic life. In man's eyes, there is nothing better than to ask the Lord to give us the strength not to do the same thing again. But in God's eyes, this is redundant, because if we have died in Christ, there is no need to make any more resolutions. We have died; our history is over and all our ideas and decisions are also over. Man always thinks that making resolutions is a good thing. But these are like reeds; they cannot fight the enemy, and they are absolutely useless before God.

BEING JOINED TO THE RESURRECTION LIFE OF CHRIST

What we have seen thus far is that God has crucified us with Christ. This alone, however, is not enough; there needs to be something more. It is that we "might be joined to another, to Him who has been raised from the dead, that we might bear fruit to God." Not only do we need a deliverance on the negative side, we also need a joining on the positive side. Without this, our work is still in vain. For this reason, God has not only crucified us on the negative side but has also joined us, who have been delivered from the law, to the resurrected Christ. Therefore, on the one side there is an exit, and on the other side there is an entrance. On the one side there is the severance, and on the other side there is the union. On the one side we are delivered from the law, and on the other side we are joined to Christ and belong to Christ. This is the resurrection that we have been speaking about. Furthermore, this is not something individual; resurrection brings all the sons into glory. John 12:24 says, "Unless the grain of wheat falls into the ground and dies, it abides alone; but if it dies, it bears much fruit." Originally there was only one life. Now this life has entered into many seeds. Originally there was only one organism. Now it has become many organisms. Originally there was only one grain of wheat. Now this grain of wheat has become many grains of wheat. In the same way, when Christ died, He dispensed His life to all the believers. In Christ, there are also two facts. The first is that we have been included in the death of Christ. When Christ died, we also died. The second is that we were resurrected with Christ. God has dispensed His life to us. This is something that every regenerated person shares in common and possesses. I do not wish to say much about this; my emphasis is on the first fact.

We who are resurrected in Christ ought to bear fruit to glorify God. God has given us the life of Christ. By this we can live out His life. The one grain that was planted is exactly the same as the thirty, sixty, or hundred grains that will spring forth. If we plant barley, surely what will come out will not be wheat or cucumber. What is planted will be the same as what grows up; there will not be a change. If what is planted is wheat, surely wheat will grow up. How then can we live a life similar to Christ's life, a life that bears fruit to glorify God? There is only one way; we must allow Christ to be lived out of us and allow Him to live. Christ has not only died for us on the cross but also lives for us within us. How can we live a life of Christ? The only way this could be done is for Christ to give His life to us. Therefore, we must have the life of Christ before we can bear fruit to glorify God.

Today I have presented to you these things before God. May we see that God has given up hope in us and considers us incurable. Although we think that there is hope and strength in us, God has given up hope in us. He has crucified us on the cross. Whenever we are outside of Christ and feel that we are still alive and able, we will immediately fall. Therefore, we can only see ourselves in Christ. When we are in Christ, there are only two facts: we have died and we have resurrected. The resurrected part is in Christ. Therefore, God wants us to live by His life. At the same time, everything that is in Adam has died. If we lay hold of this fact, we are dead to the law. Please remember that we are not only dead to the world, the self, and sin; we are also dead to the law. In this way, we will no longer have any hope for ourselves but will stand firmly in the position where God has placed us. ❧

6

A SHALLOW LIFE

"And other seed fell on the rocky place,
where it did not have much earth,
and immediately it sprang up because
it had no depth of earth."
Mark 4:5

Scripture Reading:
Song of Songs 4:12; Hosea 14:5-7; Mark 4:5-6; 16-17

Mark 4 has many important things to say concerning the Christian life. Concerning this passage, the first thing that brothers and sisters often ask is whether this passage refers to saved ones or unsaved ones. But we should not ask whether the seeds refer to saved ones or unsaved ones. The parable of the sower is not for the purpose of showing how these four kinds of soil relate to saved ones or unsaved ones. The purpose of this parable is to show us the four kinds of conditions under which man receives God's word. Therefore, it does not refer only to the word of regeneration. If it is God's word, there will be these four kinds of reactions. There will be four reactions in the case of Gentiles receiving eternal life, and there will be four reactions in the case of Christians being perfected before God. Please remember that the principle and teaching covered here have to do absolutely with the condition of the one who is receiving the word; they do not have anything to do with whether or not a person is saved. Therefore, we must not bring the issue of salvation into this passage. This passage only tells us the condition of man's receiving or refusing God's word. It is therefore applicable to the believers as well. In other words, this portion of the Scripture is not just for the Gentiles but for the Christians as well.

Now by God's grace, I will show you the kind of living that is pleasing to God and that will remain. What is the kind of living that will last and stand the tests? By God's grace, I will show you the deep degree to which God's word has to work in us before we can have the real growth in the divine word.

I know that all of us are after spirituality before God. I know that all of us desire before the Lord that we become believers who please God. We all hope that our living and work will be acceptable to God. No doubt this is what we are after. But why are there so many people who have failed along the way? Why are there so many who have only gone halfway? How many today are fully obedient to the Lord? How many are following the Lord all the way? There are many who have a good start but not many who have a good continuation. It is not surprising for anyone to have a good start. What is precious is a good continuation. A good start does not guarantee a good ending. Those who are obedient at the beginning may not be obedient at the end. When we read Leviticus, we find that those who are twenty years old are evaluated more highly than those who are sixty years old. Why? The reason is that some who were fully for the Lord when they were twenty years old retired before they were sixty. How many will follow the Lord all the way? When you were young, you were obedient. Why then have you now slackened? Perhaps a few years ago, things were not as they are now. Perhaps the heart you now have is totally different from the heart you had when you first began to follow the Lord. Perhaps some time ago, you were willing to suffer for the Lord and endure tribulations for the sake of God's will. But your condition today is different from the beginning. Is there anyone who will follow the Lord all the way and not stop halfway? Before you encounter tribulations, and before you find things contrary to your own will, it is easy to say, "Lord, I will obey You at all costs." But when the Lord's will is different from your will, when the Lord's arrangement is different from your expectation, and when you see a great mountain blocking your way and consider it too high to climb over, you will not say before the Lord, "I will obey You at all costs." This is the way many obey. In the beginning, when you see the importance of God's eternal will and the seriousness of His will with respect to Christ, you make up your mind, saying, "God, I will obey at all costs." But when God's ordained way becomes different from your way, and your expectation different from God's, you drop the necessary yoke, go around the cross that is set before you, and lose your heart to follow the Lord all the way.

Brothers and sisters, there is only one kind of life that will glorify the Lord; it is a life that bears the cross all the way to the end. Oh, we can never avoid the cross. If we are not truly dealt with by the Lord, and if we do not deny our self and take up the cross to follow Him, sooner or later we will not be able to get through. If we have not been thoroughly dealt with and have not fully consecrated ourselves once for all, there will be a day when we come face to face with something we will not be able to endure. False spiritual growth can deceive us and deceive others, but sooner or later, we will see that we cannot get through in a certain matter. A man can give up everything, but he cannot give up himself. If we are not thoroughly dealt with, we will not be able to get through in anything; we will find that the price is too great to follow the Lord and will give up.

Now we want to see the reason why some cannot follow the Lord all the way. May we find light from the Scripture, and may we receive help from God and revelation from the Holy Spirit to see this reason.

Mark 4:5 says, "And other seed fell on the rocky place, where it did not have much earth, and *immediately it sprang up* because it had no depth of earth." Immediately it sprang up. This is what happens today. To spring up is to have the hope of life. To spring up means that the seed has sprouted. To spring up means that the word is no longer just the word but has been changed to life. To spring up means that you have not only confessed the word but have received it into you; the word has begun to grow within you. To spring up means that the outer shell of the seed has been broken and the seed has sprouted. It means that you have accepted the word and made a start. Thank the Lord that we have all made a start. The word of the cross has already made a start in us. Its sprout has come forth. But the Lord said that even though some began this way, they did not have a good ending. He said, "And when the sun rose, it was scorched; and because it had no root, it withered" (v. 6). What kind of persons are these? They are the ones who have a good beginning but do not have a good ending. They are the ones who have obeyed at the beginning but have turned back halfway. What kind of persons are these? They are the ones who are willing to give up everything for the Lord at the beginning but become reluctant to do so later. They are the ones who sprang forth but have eventually dried up. They are the ones who sprang forth but are now drying up. To spring forth means that life is present; to dry up means that the hope that was present is gone. Many who failed halfway had much hope at the beginning; they knew that this way was the right way, and they expected much from this right way. Yet after three to five months, or three to five years, they are finished and dried up. The life they initially had is gone, and all the signs of life have disappeared from them.

What is the reason for this? The Lord Himself gave an explanation: "And likewise, these are the ones being sown on the rocky places, who, when they hear the word, immediately receive it with joy. Yet they have no root in themselves, but last only for a time; then when affliction or persecution occurs because of the word, immediately they are stumbled" (vv. 16-17). According to the Lord, they have met with affliction and persecution and have fallen back. The persecution spoken of here comes because of the word; it is not the ordinary kind of persecution. The affliction spoken of here comes also because of the word; it is not an ordinary kind of affliction. They received the word but cannot receive the affliction and persecution that come with the word. As a result they fall.

With every word, there is its affliction and persecution. When a Gentile, that is, a sinner, receives the Lord, spontaneously he encounters affliction and persecution. However, I will not go into that now. What I am saying is that when a Christian receives the word, any kind of word, he will surely encounter affliction and persecution. Therefore, he cannot take the word as his ornament and presume that whatever he heard, he can preach. He may be able to do this with other kinds of knowledge, but he cannot be so quick with the word. He must pass through genuine dealings, truly be dead and crucified for the word's sake, and truly broken by God for the testimony's sake before he can be a proper testimony. It is not a question of putting together a few similar verses, categorizing them a little, and composing a little to come up with a message. That is not a message. He can find many things like this in a concordance. He must be genuinely dealt with before he can have a message. Therefore, no word can be free from its accompanying affliction and persecution.

Why is this the case? After we have heard a teaching and received it, God will surely create an environment that calls for the need of that word. For example, we may hear a word on patience today and receive it. God will then create for us an environment that requires patience. Or we may hear a word on brotherly love and receive it. God will create for us an environment that requires love. What the ears hear and the mouth says is not reliable. The only thing that is genuine is being able to practice the word when things occur. This is why all the words bring their affliction and persecution. They are there to test if you have really received the word. There is not one teaching in the Bible that can be acquired without paying a price for it. Coming behind all His teachings is God's creation of an environment that calls for the need of such teachings. The purpose of this is to test if the things we have received are genuine or false.

Many times, when the brothers and sisters hear a word on the cross, a word on absolute consecration, or a word on absolute holiness, they become very excited and think that they have it, know it, and understand it. Brothers, do not rejoice so soon, for shortly thereafter affliction and persecution will come to you. They will come to test if you have indeed received this word. If you have, the affliction and persecution will prove that you have received it. If you have not received it or have only received it in a superficial or shallow way, the coming of the affliction and persecution will overwhelm you. Please remember that the affliction and persecution are there only to expose your true condition; they will never take away what is real. They only prove that you have indeed received the Lord's word; they will not cause you to lose the Lord's word. If something is gold, it will never be turned into brass through the testing of fire. No matter how hot the fire, it will not change the nature of gold. However, if something is only gilded with gold, if it is only covered with a coating of gold but does not have gold within, its nature will be exposed by the fire.

Please remember that you may hear a teaching, but the teaching is not necessarily yours. After you hear it, God will immediately give you a test to determine whether or not the word is yours. Although you have heard a word and have some scriptural knowledge about that particular word, you have not paid the price to join yourself to the word; you have not denied yourself and accepted the cross in your experience. You say with your mouth that you will obey. You may even pray happily saying, "Lord, I am willing to fully lay aside myself." Brothers and sisters, I can tell you that the Lord's sun will soon come. If you really have life, if you really have roots, and if you are genuine toward the Lord, the sun will help you to grow; it will help you with your development. But if you do not have roots, you will be dried up as soon as the sun comes out. All the trials are there to help you grow. If what you have is not genuine and not purely for the Lord, the trials will smash all that is not real and deceptive. They will show you what you really are within, exposing everything you have within and without to show you if both are the same.

Brothers and sisters, do you know what the sun is? Do you know what affliction and persecution are in reality? Let me tell you. They are the ultimate expression of the Lord's love—the cross. There is nothing that cultivates our life more than the cross, and there is no better trial than the cross. The cross has separated the whole world into two classes. On the one side are the overcoming ones, and on the other side are the defeated ones. The difference between the two is the cross. The cross makes a separation between the two. I know of many people who were just like the people in the world in the beginning; they felt happy in the world. But once they were enlightened and received God's revelation, they resolved to serve the Lord properly from that time forward. They resolved to be disciples, set aside everything else, and follow the Lord properly. They felt that they were quite good and that they could probably go on in this way. But they were deceived because they did not know their real condition. God would not allow them to be forever ignorant of their real condition. For this reason, He did something to expose their true self. They had a high evaluation of themselves, so God gave them special trials. He could not allow them to remain in darkness forever. This is why He had to give them the cross, to expose their true self. Then one day, they found that they had a problem with God and began to argue with Him. I am afraid that many Christians have already had an argument with God and developed a problem with God. One day you will find that God has not dealt with you according to your expectation. You will find that God has not done what you expected. You hope that God will do things one way, but He decides to do them another way. You hope that God will not do things that way, but He does them exactly that way. You feel unhappy and consider in your heart that God has done the wrong thing. When you see that God's speaking is different from yours, that His work is different from yours, and that the places He wants to go are different from the places you want to go, you will be dissatisfied with His arrangements and begin to argue with Him, asking why He is doing these things. You will begin to be angry with God and misunderstand Him. It may never occur to you that a servant of the Lord will encounter these things. But to your surprise, they will take hold of you. These things will not be a part of your plan, but they will fill your environment, school, home, and office. As a result, you will begin to argue with God and blame Him. Brothers and sisters, please remember that this type of argument will keep you back and make you dry. Please remember that *all of our spiritual dryness begins with arguing with God and being unwilling to yield to Him.* Every argument is followed by failures.

If God has failed, and you have won, you will surely become dry. Therefore, every time you go to God, the cross is your test; it will determine if your life is rich or dry.

I know that many of you have argued with God this way. I also know that many of you are still in the midst of arguments and have not settled them yet. You continue to complain about the way God has dealt with you. Brothers, let me tell you that the outcome of such arguments will determine how you live from this point forward. In other words, the richness or dryness of our life depends on the way you handle such arguments. If you win, God will fail, and there will be no other result but dryness. Never rejoice at your victory or your freedom. Never think that you have won forever just because you have gained what you desired. This is really a pronouncement that your life is drying up and that your living is falling fast. This is the experience of many people. All spiritual dryness comes when you begin to argue with God, when He has failed and you have won. Your life will never flourish when God fails. Actually, this will never happen. Brothers and sisters, if you are in the middle of a dispute with God and the matter is not yet settled, if there is an unresolved problem between you and God, and if you are still not clear concerning the will of God, I can frankly say that this is very dangerous. You have to be very careful. If you blame God or despise His arrangement, you will fail right then. There is no need to wait until the whole thing is exposed; your dryness will begin right then.

Therefore, God will not allow us to hear a message or offer a consecration and let the matter be concluded. Every time you say that you will not fail, that you will be an obedient Christian, and that you will follow the Lord to walk in the way, the Lord will test you immediately. The Lord will not allow you to bear the name of being obedient to Him, without first testing you. He can only use those vessels that have passed the test. Whether or not you are faithful is not determined at the time you hear a message, nor is it determined by your confession or acceptance. Since God cannot trust in you, He allows affliction and persecution pertaining to His word to come upon you and test you to see how you will react.

Then you will prove if you really are for God or if you were merely making a superficial confession. At the time of your trial, you may not praise Him as much as before. During those times, you may not be as clear about God as before. But He still has to test you.

Friends, when I first began to work for the Lord, I went one day to visit an elderly sister, Miss Barber. We sat in the living room together. She began to ask me, "Is your intention in giving yourself to serve God something that God wants? What does the Lord want you to do?" I answered, "He wants me to serve Him." She then asked, "What if the Lord does not want you to work for Him?" I answered, "He surely wants me to work for Him. I know that." She then began to read with me the passage in Matthew 15 concerning the Lord feeding the four thousand with the seven loaves and the fish. She asked me what this passage meant. I answered that the disciples put the loaves and the fish in the Lord's hand, and when the Lord had blessed them, they became manifold and the four thousand were fed. She then added one word, which I can never forget to this day. Of course, at that time I was quite bewildered. She said that all the loaves in the Lord's hand were first broken before they were distributed. Any loaf that was not broken could not be changed and could not sustain another's life. She also said, "Brother (actually she was older than my parents), please remember that many times we are like the loaves, who would say: 'Lord, I will consecrate myself to you.' But even though we have consecrated ourselves, we secretly hope in our heart that the Lord will not break us. We hope that the loaf can always be whole, beautiful, and always remain unchanged. But no loaf that is in His hand is ever unbroken. If you do not want to be broken, it is better that you do not put yourself in His hand." It has been twelve years since the day she talked to me about this. During these twelve years, I have deeply learned this lesson. I realize deeply that this word is true. Every loaf that is in the Lord's hand is broken by Him. Therefore, allow me to say the same thing to you now: "If you do not want to be broken by the Lord, please do not put yourself into His hand." This is where the problem lies with many people. When they hear the teachings concerning overcoming, they are very happy and say,

"God, I will consecrate everything I have to you." But when God begins to break them, they cry, "Oh, I did not expect to encounter such things." Brothers and sisters, this kind of living is painful and difficult to bear. On the one hand, God has laid hold of us, and we cannot be like other ordinary men anymore. On the other hand, we do not want to be broken that way. Therefore, if you have not counted the cost and are not ready to be broken by Him, you will find yourselves dissatisfied with God, and God will be dissatisfied with you.

If you do not want to follow the Lord, God can do nothing with you. But if you realize that it is right to obey the Lord and do not want your life to dry up, wanting instead to have a strong and vigorous life, you will have to allow God to test the reality of the word you received with affliction and persecution. I do not know how many people have experienced dryness as a result of failing the test of this word.

In another two days, we will consider God's eternal purpose. It is questionable whether or not we can come up to that standard. Many times we hope and desire, but we have not passed through the dealings in a proper way. As a result, we cannot be as we wish. Therefore, the cross is our test. The cross will separate us, and we will see on which side we are. I will not go into this at this time. I will speak on the reason that the seed becomes dry. Why do seeds grow so fast, yet dry up so soon? Why do they dry up immediately after the sun comes out? The Lord gives us three reasons in Mark 4.

NOT HAVING ENOUGH EARTH

He said that the first reason is that there is not enough earth. This means that the earth is not deep; there is not much depth to the earth. A person in this condition has just a small amount; everything about him is shallow. There is not much within him; he is very superficial. He is easily satisfied and easily hungry. He takes in little and is satisfied with a little. It is easy for him to rejoice and easy for him to be sorrowful. It is easy for him to laugh and easy for him to cry. He is standing in a shallow place. He is a person living according to his environment, that is, he lives in his emotions. There is nothing in this world that is more shallow than his emotion and environment.

If a tree is large, its roots will surely be big, because it has to go deep into the earth to find water. Some roots go down as far as two or three miles because there is no water on the surface. When roots find no water on the surface, they will go to the depths. They will go down miles for water. One can find palm trees in the middle of the Arabian deserts. They wave with lush greenness under the scorching sun. The reason they can do this is that their roots have stretched themselves to the sweet water; they are no longer afraid of the hot sun. Therefore, even though they are most severely burned, they can absorb the cool water freely because they are not living on the surface of the earth but within the depths of the soil.

Oh, all those who live by their environment or by their feelings are living on shallow ground. Although I have not been working for the Lord for a long time, according to my experience, the most difficult kind of people are those who say "yes" to everything. No matter what you say, they respond with "yes," superficially accepting what you say. They appear to be very attentive. Actually, within them, they have nothing. The people who laugh and cry easily, who are easily affected by the weather, who become happy or sad because of their feelings or environment, are difficult to handle. The people of shallow earth are controlled by their emotions or environment. The deep ones are not that way. What they see is not the environment, but the Lord behind the environment. What they know is not the emotion. They have locked up their emotion and know the Lord *from within.*

Brothers and sisters, what becomes of those with a little earth? The Lord shows us a profound lesson here. If we are not looking at the Lord behind the environment but are living by our emotion or the environment, we will not be able to hold fast to any doctrine or teaching. What is the Lord doing among us today? He is seeking for some among us to be the overcomers. We will never be able to be the overcomers if we live every day according to the environment without any assurance at all; this is to live by our feelings without the knowledge of the Lord. Many Christians are happy when they progress in a smooth way. But when they encounter any darkness, they feel that everything is depressing. They do not know anything about the work of the Holy Spirit. They are not living by the Lord, but by man's word, their own thoughts, and the arrangement of the environment. If they live this way, they will immediately fail when the trials come. Once the cross comes to them, they will fall. Therefore, if we fall back at the trials and do not take up the cross to press on, we will not be of much use to the Lord. Rather, we will be shallow, without much of anything, sensitive in our feelings, and living according to our feelings.

HAVING NO ROOT

The Lord tells us that the second reason for barrenness is the lack of roots. What is a root? In a tree, the part that can be seen is the trunk, while the part beneath the ground, which cannot be seen, is the root. The branches have life and are visible; the roots are invisible. The roots are buried in the earth. Therefore, the roots refer to the *hidden life*. Those who do not have any root before the Lord will be dried up in their life. Those who do not have a hidden life, who do everything before men and have nothing special before the Lord, cannot stand the test of the cross. Brothers and sisters, let me ask you honestly, is your living only what is seen by men? Do you have any secret life before the Lord, inside your own room? If your prayers can only be heard in the prayer meetings, if you only read your Bible to others, and if your works are all before men, you do not have any roots. Do you know what the roots are? The roots are the parts that cannot be seen, that are hidden, and that are in secret. The visible parts are not the roots. Therefore, before the Lord you must ask yourself how much of your living is actually before Him? Other than the part of your living, testimony, Bible reading, and prayer that have been done before men, how much has been done in secret? If you do not have a secret or hidden life before God and if you do not have any secret prayer, reading, or obedience, I can say very frankly that you do not have any roots. When the cross comes, it is no wonder that you cannot bear it. The only reason for this is that you lack a crucial, hidden life. Nothing can preserve you as much as a hidden life. If you see that a brother has fallen or failed, or has come into trouble, without asking anyone, you can surely say that prior to this trouble he lost his hidden life. He lost his hidden life during the previous weeks, months, or even years. Your spiritual life depends very much on your hidden life before God. If you cannot sustain a hidden life, you will be weak before the Lord. Therefore, you should realize the importance of the hidden life.

The shutting of the door in Matthew is a kind of root life. What did the Lord say in verse 6:6? He said that when we pray, we should enter into a private room, shut the door, and pray to the Father who is in secret, and the Father who sees in secret will repay us. The Lord is very particular; He said that the Father will *see* us in secret. Prayer is something that can be seen. We have always thought that prayer is something that is heard; however, the Lord did not say that prayers are heard, but that prayers are seen. Many times when we have no words before the Lord, our attitude alone is precious enough, because God is seeing and not just hearing us. Brothers and sisters, how much of what we are can be seen before God? How much of our living can be seen by God? How many times are we only seen by the Lord and no one else? Or are we doing everything in front of men? Now I have to say a few words particularly to the brothers who are co-workers. No one is as susceptible as the Lord's workers. We suffer more temptations than others, because it is easier for us to put everything before men; we can even display what we have in secret. Brothers, let me ask again, how much of our lives are seen by God alone and not known by men? How much of our lives are spiritual before God and have never been told to men? How many of us have the experience of Paul, who hid his experience for fourteen years? How many of our things are kept exclusively for God's enjoyment? If we do not have anything like this, I can honestly say that we do not have any roots. If we do not have a hidden spiritual life and have not been dealt with by God or smitten by Him in a hidden way, everything will be superficial and of no account.

Everything that man has must first be properly tested on the cross and able to stand the test before it can be considered reliable. If a man is deeply rooted in the death of Christ, he may go through trials, but he will still stand. Let me ask you this question: would you still say that you believe, if you are being persecuted for the Lord's sake to the point of death, with someone saying, "I will kill you if you continue to believe in Jesus"? How do you know that you would not fall back in an attempt to spare your own life? The only protection you have when you go through trials, tribulations, and persecution is to have deep roots. If the roots are not deep, you will surely fail. If the roots are not deep, you will not be able to be an overcomer. If you want to remain standing in that day, you must have deep roots in ordinary times. This means that you must have a hidden life before the Lord and must continually have hidden experiences. Therefore, the only way that we can know that we will not fall in that day is by having an adequate amount of hidden life today.

THE ROCKY PLACE

Those with shallow earth may still have a desire for deep roots, but there are rocks that block the way. There are rocks where the roots are. They may outwardly look the same as other soil; just like others, they are filled with dust and mud. But within there are hidden sins and the self. Outwardly, they look the same as everyone else. They can listen as others listen and speak as others speak. But in hidden places, big rocks block the way. This is why they cannot be deep. What are the rocks? In the Bible, rocks have many meanings. I can only mention one today, the hardened heart. If you want to be spiritual, you must not have a hardened heart. Many people have never received a blow to their will; their self has never been broken before God. They can say a great deal about God's will and provide many reasonings. They always have their own ideas about God's will. They always say *I think* that something should be done this way or that way. God has not yet destroyed their wisdom, nor torn down their will. They are still scheming and planning, but there are rocks underneath, so they cannot go deep. Brothers and sisters, allow me to say an honest word: we cannot have real spiritual progress unless we allow ourselves to be broken by God. The cross is our only source of progress. If God does not break us, we will never become useful. He must break the rocks beneath us. Otherwise, we will never be deep. Only one kind of people will go all the way down to the depths; they are the ones who are as soft as a child. Only one kind of people can take firm roots; they are the ones who fear and tremble at God's word. Unfortunately, a countless number of people have to think before they will make a decision concerning God's command! They think that God's command requires discernment and selection. Thank the Lord that there are also many here who have obeyed in a very simple way. Thank the Lord that there are many who only care "who" is giving the command and never question "why" before they obey. Brothers and sisters, a disobedient heart is a rock. May God shine His light on us, so that we may see the enormity of the rock within us.

The rocks are not only your self; they are your hidden sins. In your life there is always one sin which has not been removed because of the high price; it remains there, and you are reluctant to remove it. If you leave it there, you will never receive spiritual riches; you will never go deeper because of it. Therefore, you have to deal thoroughly with your sins. Even the hidden sins have to be dealt with thoroughly. If you have not dealt thoroughly with the hidden sins, and if the stubborn self is not thoroughly dealt with, your roots will never be deep.

Brothers and sisters, how many things has God pointed His finger at in you? Are you unwilling to look at Him? Are you fighting and refusing to surrender? Perhaps there is already a problem between you and God. Perhaps you have seen God's will and are debating with Him. This is what the Lord wants to show you today. Brothers, if you really want to serve Him and acquire the truth before Him, the large rocks must be removed. Otherwise, the earth will always be shallow, and the roots will not be deep. If you cannot remove the hidden sins, the stubborn self, and the opinions that are expressed as "I don't want to" and "I will not," you will never acquire any spiritual power. If there is a problem between you and God, it will be impossible for the earth to have any depth or the roots to be deep. Thank the Lord that in spite of this, He can still do His work. Your heart is hardened, but the Lord can change you. I know that many people here have been smitten by God before. But I also know that there are many here who are quite stubborn. However, if the Lord can break others, He can also break you. If the Lord was able to sit on a donkey that had never been sat on when He entered Jerusalem, He can sit on you as well. Anyone who has ever sat on a donkey knows that a donkey that has never been sat on is the most difficult kind. But the Lord could do it. He could very safely sit on that donkey and enter Jerusalem. In the same way, He can sit on you. Although you are very stubborn before God, the Lord can break you, no matter how stubborn you are. You should sincerely pray today, "Lord, I am really hard within. Many times I have held onto my own will and have insisted on my own opinions. That is why so many times, I have been a shallow person. Please break me." We do not know how shallow our life is before God. If we allow God to break our hardened heart, if we do not live by our feelings or the environment, and if we ask God to give us more of a hidden life, we will see forward progress. If we deal thoroughly with every cross that comes our way and take up the cross every time it comes, we will become deeper and deeper, moment by moment.

Although we have read two other passages of Scripture, I cannot cover them in detail today. I can only speak about them briefly because there is not much time left, and I have already covered much of what I wanted to speak. Let us cover these passages just a little to make up for what we have missed. In Hosea 14 Lebanon is mentioned three times. First, it is mentioned in contrast to the lily. Second, it is mentioned in contrast to the olive tree. Third, it is mentioned in contrast to the vine. Lebanon is repeatedly mentioned; there is Lebanon in contrast to the lily, Lebanon in contrast to the olive tree, and Lebanon in contrast to the vine. Lebanon is repeatedly mentioned because there is a kind of cedar tree in Lebanon. Cedar trees are tall trees with very deep roots. Very few trees have roots as deep as the cedar tree. The Bible considers the cedar trees of Lebanon to be the greatest trees in the world. They signify those who will take deep roots. Do not treasure what the world says to you, because the Bible shows that the Lord is only pleased with those who have roots that go downward.

In this passage the Lord shows us three things. First, He made a contrast between the lily and Lebanon. Second, He made a contrast between the olive tree and Lebanon. Third, He made a contrast between the vine and Lebanon. Why does the Lord make a contrast between the lily and Lebanon? He makes the contrast because the lily is very attractive. Christians should not have flowers that are grown in gardens, but in the valley. Lilies grow in the wilderness, not in homes. They grow in the valley and do not need gardeners to cultivate them. Rather, they are sustained by water from heaven; they are fully cultivated and sustained by God. The beauty of the lily lies in the wilderness; it lies before God. Hosea 14:6 says also that Israel's splendor shall be as the olive tree. According to my consideration, there is absolutely no beauty in the olive tree. It would be more plausible and real to say that its beauty shall be as the peony. Saying that its beauty shall be as the olive tree does not seem too appropriate. However, God's beauty is not in appearance but in fruit. We know that the olive tree is a tree bearing fruit for oil; it is a tree that bears the fruit of the Spirit. The beauty of the olive tree lies in its fruit, which typifies the Spirit. This is something inward; it is not something that appears before men. Further on, it says that Israel shall grow as the vine. I do not know how many of you have seen blossoms on a vine. We have grown a vine in our home every year since my youth. But I have never seen anyone putting vine blossoms in a vase, and I have never seen vine blossoms. Unless you look for them carefully, you cannot find the blossoms; the blossoms are as small as specks of dust. Before they have fully blossomed, they become grapes. Why does it not say peach blossoms or plum blossoms instead of vine blossoms? The one reason is that our flower is not for beauty, but for fruit-bearing. There are three kinds of flowers in this world. One is for display only, like the chrysanthemum flower. Another is both for display and for fruit, like the plum blossom. The third is for fruit-bearing alone, like the blossoms on the vine. God has no intention that we be like the plum blossom or chrysanthemum flower, which are for display. God has only one requirement: we have to have roots that go downward. Lebanon is mentioned three times, and each time we are told to take care of the hidden life. This is very crucial. Perhaps a life that bears spiritual fruit does not look that good. The prayer life is not something that looks good. However, we are living to God and as long as God considers it to be good, that is enough.

A similar passage is found in the Song of Solomon 4:12, which says, "A garden enclosed is my sister, my bride, // A spring shut up, a fountain sealed." [The word *spring* is translated "well" in the Chinese Union Version.] A garden enclosed means that it is not a public garden; it is not a garden into which everyone can go. Rather, it is a garden enclosed, reserved for special ones. The flower in our garden is set apart for Christ and is not for anyone else. Not everyone can see it. "A well shut up." There is a difference between a well and fountain. A well is something man-made, while a fountain is something natural. Abraham always dug wells. Whenever his servants found a source, he dug a well. However, a fountain is natural and has not been worked on by man. The Lord says that we are a garden enclosed and that we are not open at any other time; the only time we are open is when we open to the Lord. We are also a well shut up. A well is for man's use. However, even though it is for man's use, it is still limited by the Lord and shut up for Him. The fountain signifies what we have received from God; it signifies the joy we have received from the Lord. The well is before man, while the fountain is before God. None of these can be shown to others purposely; they are all concealed. All of our experiences in prayer should be concealed and not made public. Even the part that is for man is concealed. In short, all the good things that we possess should be locked up for the Lord.

All of the speaking today concerns only one thing, that is, to go "down." We have no goal other than allowing the cross to do a deeper work in us. Brothers and sisters, there are too many superficial and shallow things. There are too many things growing outside, exposed on the surface, and seen only by man. What is lacking is a hidden part before God. What God is seeking today and the one thing that grips our heart, is a hidden life before Him, something invisible to man. The life that God wants is like the life of a sister, a life that is hidden in the background. God has no intention that we put everything on the outside and have nothing hidden and secret. May God grant us the grace to accept His demands and not be as we were before. May we ask and allow God to grant us a real breaking so that we can go on in the way ahead. ❋

7

WHAT ARE WE?

"They said then to him, Who are you,
that we may give an answer to those who sent us?
What do you say about yourself?"
John 1:22

"Therefore I will be ready always to remind you
concerning these things, even though you know them and have
been established in the present truth."
2 Peter 1:12

Scripture Reading:
John 1:22; 2 Peter 1:12

Today we will look at one question: what are we? What are we doing here? In the past we have not said much about this matter because it is somewhat awkward to do so. For this reason we have been reluctant to speak about ourselves. However, though we have not mentioned the matter, others have often asked us, "What are you?" Some have even said that we are the Revival Church, or the Little Flock Church, or The Christian [Editor's note: Watchman Nee published a magazine, *The Christian*] Church. Hence, we would like to say a few words concerning this question.

First, we must clarify that we are not some thing. We are not a new denomination. Neither are we a new sect, a new movement, or a new organization. We are not here to join a certain sect or form our own sect. Other than having a special calling and commission from God, there would be no need for us to exist independently. The reason we are here is that God has given us a special calling.

ESTABLISHED IN THE PRESENT TRUTH

Second Peter 1:12 mentions the words "established in the present truth." The "present truth" can also be rendered the "up-to-date truth." What is the up-to-date truth? Actually, all the truths are in the Bible; there is not one truth that is not in the Bible. Although they are all in the Bible, through man's foolishness, unfaithfulness, negligence, and disobedience many of the truths were lost and hidden from man. The truths were there, but man did not see them or touch them. Not until the fullness of time did God release certain truths during particular periods of time and cause them to be revealed once more.

These freshly revealed truths are not God's new inventions. Rather, they are man's new discoveries. There is no need for invention, but there is the need for discovery. In past generations God revealed different truths. During certain periods of time, He caused men to discover these specific truths. We can see this clearly from the history of the church.

Take, for example, the raising up of Martin Luther in the sixteenth century. God opened his eyes to see the matter of justification by faith. He was a vessel raised up by God to unveil the truth of justification by faith. This does not mean that before Luther there was no such thing as justification by faith. The fact already existed before Luther's time. Luther was merely the one who realized this truth in a stronger way; he was particularly outstanding in this truth. For this reason, this truth became the "present truth" in that age.

Every worker of the Lord should inquire before God as to what the present truth is. We need to ask: "God, what is the present truth?" Although there are many major and crucial truths in the Bible, what we need to know is God's present truth. Not only do we need to know the general truths, we must also be clear about God's present truth.

TRUTH RECOVERED DURING THE SIXTEENTH CENTURY

From the sixteenth century on, God has been recovering different truths. The sixteenth century was the age of the Reformation. It was a time of monumental change in religion. This does not mean that before the sixteenth century there was no recovery. There were recoveries before that time. However, it was from the sixteenth century on that there were significant recoveries. We have to consider the history from the time of the Reformation as belonging to four periods. The first period is the period of the Reformation. The second period is the time immediately after the Reformation, from the sixteenth century to the eighteenth century. The third period is the nineteenth century, and the last period is the present twentieth century.

First, let us consider Luther's Reformation. When Luther was raised up by God, he saw the light and proposed that man go back to the truth in the book of Romans. Today many people evaluate Luther's work from the political angle and consider it to be a political movement. However, having read Luther's diaries, writings, and books, I see that his motives and goals were right. The best thing about him was his recovery of the truth of justification by faith. This is Luther's particular recovery. Of course, God did not recover all the truths through Luther. Luther recovered only the truth concerning justification by faith. He did not make complete changes with regard to the church. For example, he still recognized the state church and approved of the church being part of the state. He did not receive light regarding this point. For this reason, not long after, the Lutheran denomination became the state religion of Germany. Luther himself once said that the church should not be controlled by the state. Yet he considered administrative questions transitional, temporal, and of the outer court, and not matters that belong to the Holy Place. Therefore, he was not thorough in this matter. God allowed the question of church administration to be left unsolved at Luther's time. Although this matter was not successfully recovered, the truth of justification by faith was definitely recovered. God dug up this buried truth from all the traditions, human opinions, and creeds and caused this truth to be known and preached once more. If a person were born in that age, what he should have done was preach this truth and exhort others concerning this truth. If he did not do this, he should not be considered a faithful worker of God in that age.

THE RECOVERY OF TRUTH FROM THE SIXTEENTH TO THE EIGHTEENTH CENTURY

Following this we come to the period from the sixteenth to the eighteenth century. In 1524 the Anabaptists, a group of believers who proposed re-baptism after infant-sprinkling, were raised up in Germany. They were followers of the earlier brothers from Lhota who preached the baptism of believers. Before this time the Roman Catholic Church as well as the Lutheran Church sprinkled infants. These Anabaptists not only preached the truth of justification by faith, but they went on further to baptize the believers who were justified by faith. After the Anglican Church was established in England, these people told others that the church should not have anything to do with politics. For this reason they were persecuted and exiled.

After twelve years, in 1536 John Calvin was raised up by God. He was one of the greatest vessels of God in that age. After he was raised up, he faced persecution everywhere, first in Switzerland and then in Germany. Wherever he went, he was met with persecution and exile. Finally, in Scotland he had a fresh beginning and established the Scottish Presbyterian Church.

The period between the end of the sixteenth century and the beginning of the seventeenth century was the time the Anglican Church was formed in England. This was the beginning of the state church in England. Although it freed itself from the influence of the Roman Catholic Church, it found itself linked with British politics. For this reason, various dissenters rose up in England. They opposed the state religion and held opinions different from those of the state religion. They said that the church should not be under the state's control and that church and state should have a clear separation. Although these dissenters were bold to point out the mistakes of the state church, they themselves did not return fully to the teaching of the New Testament. These are the things that happened in England.

At this time in Germany, God raised up Philipp Jakob Spener. He became a pastor in a Lutheran Church in Frankfurt in 1670. By that time the Lutheran denomination had fallen into a kind of formal religion. By reading his Bible, Spener found out that the church at his time was full of human opinions, something forbidden by God. He saw that the believers should return to the teaching of the New Testament. For this reason he began to lead others into the practice of 1 Corinthians 14. In his meetings he began to teach others to reject the traditional formalities and to follow the leading of the Holy Spirit. Unfortunately, his practice did not last long.

By 1732 the earliest missionary body in the world was conceived, the so-called Moravian Brethren. The word *Moravian* originates from a place called Moravia. They were the first group of brothers to go throughout the entire world to evangelize. Eighty-five out of one hundred among them eventually became foreign missionaries. Their beginning can be traced to a brother called Christian David. He was regenerated at the age of twenty-two. Before he was saved, he had traveled everywhere in search of the truth concerning salvation but to no avail. One day he found the way to salvation. After he was saved, he returned to his hometown in Moravia and began to boldly proclaim this truth. God did a great work through him. Through this revival, persecution came, and he was chased out of his homeland to Saxony. There he met Count Zinzendorf. The latter was only twenty-two years of age at that time and was a member of the aristocracy in a small kingdom. Due to the persecution in Moravia, the brothers fled from their land and were received by Brother Zinzendorf in his territory. There they began the Moravian Church. Dwelling among the little hills of Saxony, they began to build up a homeland. Gradually different kinds of Christians moved there from their respective places of persecution.

Among these immigrants was a black man from the West Indies by the name of Anthony. After he came to meet the brothers, he discussed with them the condition in the West Indies. Some brothers felt the need to go and preach the gospel there. Through the casting of lots, they selected a few workers to go with Anthony on a mission. This was the first foreign missionary enterprise, around 1732. From that time on, missionaries were produced from among them, and the Moravian Church became the strongest missionary body at that time. Their believers spread to every corner of the world.

At the same time there was a new discovery within the Catholic Church. A group of spiritual people were raised up by the Lord. The most spiritual one among them was Miguel de Molinos, who was born in 1640 and died in 1697. He wrote a book called *Spiritual Guide* which taught men the way to deny themselves and die with the Lord. This book affected many people at that time. One of his contemporaries was Madame Guyon. She was born in 1648 and died in 1717. She was even more knowledgeable in the matters of the union with God's will and the denial of the self. Her autobiography is a very good spiritual book.

In addition there was Father Fenelon who was a bishop at that time. He was very willing to suffer for the Lord, and he worked together with Madame Guyon. Through these men and women, God released many spiritual messages. At that time men and women with the deepest experience of spiritual life were found in the Catholic Church. Protestantism was only paying attention to the doctrine of justification by faith.

Along with these three persons, there was Gottfried Arnold. He wrote many books concerning questions of the church. He considered that the church at that time had deviated from the truth and that it must return to the proper ground as revealed in the New Testament before it could be built up. Here we can see two flows. One came from believers like Molinos, Madame Guyon, and Fenelon. The other flow came from men represented by Arnold. In our magazine, *The Present Testimony,* we have published Madame Guyon's "Flow of the Spirit." Through her writings, one can see that she was indeed a very spiritual person. Concerning Arnold, he recovered mostly the outward matters. He proposed that Christians return to the scriptural ground of the New Testament.

These two flows eventually merged into one. In 1700 the church in "Philadelphia" was raised up. Philadelphia means brotherly love. At that time, when men read Revelation 2 and 3, they realized that Protestantism had indeed come out of Catholicism. However, the result was only the church in Sardis; there was not yet a full recovery.

When such groups were raised up, unlike other organizations, they did not call people to come out of their original organizations. They did not insist that others leave their denominations. On the contrary, they merely held meetings everywhere. From 1670 on, their testimony was found in England. In Leeds, Bradford, and other places, their meetings were raised up one after another. They were the strongest witnesses in the eighteenth century. While Zinzendorf was still alive, he tried once to absorb this movement into his Moravian Church. However, he did not succeed.

At the beginning of the eighteenth century, a great revival broke out in England. In 1729 the two Wesley brothers were raised up by God. They were called the Methodists. Through them, God brought in a great tide of revival. This was the beginning of the Methodist Church. The Wesley brothers were the prime figures of the eighteenth century. Before John Wesley was saved, he strove to be good. Later he went to America to be a missionary. At that point he was not yet saved. He testified that although he had heard the truth of justification by faith, he could not understand it. Later a Moravian brother helped him and told him, "Just preach justification by faith to others until you yourself are assured that you are justified by faith." A short while after this, he was saved. After their salvation, the two brothers immediately began to preach this message everywhere. At that time men were not allowed to preach in the open air but could speak only in a church sanctuary because the church at that time considered that the holy Word could be proclaimed only in a holy sanctuary. However, these two brothers together with George Whitefield began to hold open-air meetings and bring people to the Lord in this way. The main subject of John Wesley's messages was the doctrine of sanctification. The teaching of the eradication of sin began with him, although he also told others that sanctification came by faith.

After Wesley died, the overseas missionary movement began. The first organization to be established was the London Missionary Society. This organization began as a non-denominational institution but later came under the direction of the Congregationalists. By 1799 the Church Missionary Society (C.M.S.) was formed. It belonged to the Anglican Church. The Methodists also expanded the scope of their mission organization and became the Methodist Missionary Society of today.

In conclusion, the reforms of the sixteenth century were widespread, while the reforms of the eighteenth century were not. The reforms of the sixteenth century affected the world not only spiritually but politically and socially as well. Those reforms of the eighteenth century exercised their influence mainly on the spiritual side. Of all the movements in the eighteenth century, the most noteworthy was the testimony of the "Philadelphia" church. They assimilated all of the previous major recoveries. Among them, one can find all of the major truths.

THE DISCOVERY OF GOD'S TRUTH IN THE NINETEENTH CENTURY

Now let us consider the nineteenth century. This century saw a full revival. First, we will consider John Nelson Darby and the revival that he represented.

In 1827 a group of people were raised up in Dublin, Ireland. Among them were men like Edward Cronin and Anthony Norris Groves. They saw that many things in the church were dead, lifeless, and formal. They began to ask the Lord to show them the church according to the biblical revelation. Through prayer and fellowship, they felt that they should rise up and meet according to the principle of 1 Corinthians 14. As a result, they began to break bread at a brother's home. A short while later, a former Anglican minister, John Nelson Darby, began to join their meeting and to expound the Bible among them. Gradually, more and more expositors were raised up among them, such as William Kelly, C. H. Mackintosh, B. W. Newton, and J. G. Bellett. Through reading their books, I received light to see the error of denominational organizations and to realize that there is only one Body of Christ. The church should not be formed by human opinions but should be under the direct leading of the Holy Spirit. When we consider the present-day church organizations, we see many human traditions and opinions and little direct leading of the Holy Spirit. This is not according to God's desire. In God's will, the church should not be under man's control; it should be directed only by the Holy Spirit. All those who belong to the Lord should learn to be led by the Holy Spirit and should not follow man's direction. These are all truths discovered by the Brethren.

In addition, the Brethren made many discoveries concerning the millennium, the question of rapture, and the prophecies in Daniel and Revelation. They were the most prominent expositors of the various types in the Old Testament. The commentary on the Pentateuch by C. H. Mackintosh is the authority in its category. The evangelist D. L. Moody highly recommended it. The Brethren also made a clear separation between the biblical prophecies concerning the Jews and those concerning the church. A hundred years ago, many people confused the prophecies concerning the Jews with those for the church. They considered that the prophecies concerning the Jews were already fulfilled in the church. In addition to these matters, the Brethren also produced many other writings.

During this period, many spiritual brothers were being raised up in England. In addition to those named above, there were brothers like Charles Stanley and George Cutting. The latter wrote a little book called *Safety, Certainty, and Enjoyment.* It tells people that they can have the assurance of salvation. This book has already been translated into Chinese. The truths concerning the gospel were fully recovered through these brothers.

Besides these brothers there was Robert Govett who saw the

matter of Christian reward. He discovered that while it is true that a man is saved by faith, he is rewarded according to his works before God. Salvation is a matter of life, while reward is a matter of living. C. H. Spurgeon once said that Govett was a hundred years ahead of his time because his teachings were so profound. Govett told people that there is the possibility that Christians will be excluded from the millennium. Therefore, a believer must be faithful and diligent. Second, he taught that not all believers will be raptured before the tribulation. Only those overcoming and faithful believers will participate in this rapture.

Expositors were raised up one after another during this period. Another very spiritual brother of great renown was G. H. Pember. He wrote many commentaries. There were others also such as D. M. Panton and Hudson Taylor. The latter wrote a book *Union and Communion,* which speaks of some profound experiences in Christ. The above-mentioned truths were all great discoveries. Although these different truths of God were recovered, they cannot be considered God's most central truth.

Afterward God raised up George Müller in England. He learned many excellent lessons concerning prayer and concerning faith in God's word. He taught that man should claim God's promises through prayer, and he testified of his way of living by faith in relation to financial needs.

In the United States there was the Christian and Missionary Alliance. The prominent ones among them were A. B. Simpson, A. J. Gordon, and others. They were all very influential. Even Hudson Taylor in England was affected by them. They saw that believers should return to the experience of the apostolic age when men lived by faith. This was a tremendous revelation at that time. Of course, this truth has become widely known among us today.

Gordon and Simpson also discovered the truth concerning divine healing and began to experience it. This matter spread quickly and was much publicized, and many were attracted. However, Simpson emphasized that it was not the healing but the resurrection life that overcame the weaknesses of the flesh. He taught that one can triumph over sickness through knowing Christ as the power and the Deliverer.

At the same time another group of people were raised up who paid attention to the inner life. About sixty years ago, God gained a porcelain merchant by the name of Robert Pearsall Smith. He saw that sanctification comes through consecration. This kind of sanctification is quite different from the sanctification that Wesley spoke of. Smith's kind of sanctification came through consecration and faith. The sanctification that Wesley preached was a life that one gradually attains to after consecration. Actually, both teachings are of the truth. After the line of Smith, there was Mrs. Hannah Whitall Smith who wrote the book *The Christian's Secret of a Happy Life*. There were also others like Stocknell (?), Evan Hopkins, and Andrew Murray. They continued the line of truth concerning self-denial preached by ones like Madame Guyon two hundred years earlier in the Catholic Church. These believers began to conduct conferences in Germany, England, and other places. These conferences were the beginning of what we know today as the Keswick Convention. The main speaker at these conventions was Evan Hopkins. He received help both from Smith and from others like Madame Guyon and exerted a definite spiritual influence in that period of time. Although the truth released by Madame Guyon has never been popular throughout church history, it has exercised a profound spiritual influence upon many people. Even Wesley received help from her. John Wesley once said that he wished every believer would read the messages of Madame Guyon and that he owed much grace to her. God gained such a woman in the seventeenth century and through her brought in the main current of the nineteenth century.

In addition to Hopkins, there was H. C. Trumbull who released the truth on the overcoming life at the Keswick Convention. These messages brought in a great recovery concerning the knowledge of the overcoming life and the way for believers to experience this overcoming life in their living.

After Hopkins, God gained another sister, Mrs. Jessie Penn-Lewis. This sister was very weak physically during the early stages of her life. She was always bedridden. While sick in bed, she read the writings of Madame Guyon and embraced them as her bedside companion. She, however, could not believe that the kind of total self-denial, faith, and love described in these writings could ever be practiced. One day while disputing and arguing with God, she sought desperately for the Lord to bring her into these truths. The Lord heard her prayer. From that time on, she was raised up by the Lord to preach the truth of the cross.

Brother Holden, an ex-missionary of the China Inland Mission, came to know the meaning of the cross through reading Mrs. Penn-Lewis's books. Mrs. Penn-Lewis was one who truly bore the cross. Through her experiences, many believers were attracted to pursue the truth concerning the cross. Through these men and women, God led many to realize that the centrality of God's work is the cross. The cross is the foundation for all spiritual matters. Without the work of the cross, a person will not know what is death and what is sin. Many spiritual persons received great help through her. Through the messages she preached, God granted deliverance to many. We can see that the discovery of God's truth is progressive; the more it advances, the more complete it becomes. By the end of the nineteenth century, almost all of the truths had been recovered.

THE ADVANCE OF TRUTH IN THE TWENTIETH CENTURY

Now we come to the twentieth century. Two great events occurred in the twentieth century. The first was the Chinese Boxer Rebellion of 1900. During this rebellion many Christians were martyred. The second event was the great Welsh Revival of 1904. During this revival many towns saw their whole population saved to such an extent that there were no more souls to save. Many phenomena of Pentecost were manifested among them.

The leader of this revival was Evan Roberts, a twenty-two-year-old coal miner. He had not received much education. God called such a one from among the lowly and gave him a partner,

Hastwell (?). After he was saved, Roberts often prayed earnestly in the coal mines. His only prayer was, "Lord, bend the church to save the world." Those around him were both bewildered as well as impressed. Gradually, more people joined him in prayer, and soon the entire mine was affected. Many miners rose up to pray. The revival began to spread to the entire region of southern England.

From them we have learned two truths: first, the revival work of the Holy Spirit is brought in through a group of people who are bent and subdued. We do not need to ask God to send us an outward revival. We only need to ask Him to subdue us in a deeper and fresher way. Then life will spontaneously flow out from our being.

Second, from this time on, many began to understand the work of the evil spirits. Before this time, although men talked about this subject, their knowledge of it was not thorough. Brother Roberts understood what spiritual warfare meant. The experience of Ephesians 6 was not thoroughly apprehended until his time. In 1908 while he was lying on his sickbed, he told of his experience of warfare with the evil spirits to Mr. and Mrs. Penn-Lewis. Based on this understanding and the latter's personal experience, she wrote the book *War on the Saints* which helped many deceived believers become free. During the past few years, almost all of the messages talked about among spiritual believers have been the teachings of Mrs. Penn-Lewis. They are truths concerning spiritual warfare and the cross.

At the same time that this revival was going on, another new work began in Los Angeles in the United States. From 1908 to 1909, a number of black believers on Azusa Street experienced the baptism of the Holy Spirit and began to speak in tongues. Concerning tongue-speaking, it is true that the practice among many is extreme and improper. Of course, we do not nullify altogether the place of tongue-speaking. We should help others have this Pentecostal experience. Paul's teaching was, on the one hand, that not all speak in tongues (1 Cor. 12:30). On the other hand, he told us, "Do not forbid the speaking in tongues" (14:39). The first verse is for those who overemphasize this matter. The second verse is for those who overlook this matter. We should take note of both aspects.

These individuals saw that the prophecy of Joel 2 was only partially fulfilled at the time of the apostles and that the day of the latter rain must come before the complete fulfillment occurs. Spiritually speaking, "the day of the latter rain" refers to today.

GOD'S WORK TODAY AND THE CUMULATIVE REVELATIONS OF GOD

From the above discussion we can see the different discoveries of God's truths that took place before and during this century. Now we need to ask: what is God's work in China today? What kind of work is God doing today?

Immediately after I was saved, I heard many teachings from the foreign missionaries. Prior to 1920 it was difficult in China even to hear a message on salvation. After 1920 many messages were preached concerning salvation, justification, and regeneration. Before that time, many people did not even know about salvation. At present there are over one hundred and fifty different kinds of denominations. God showed us the error of denominationalism and the mistake of sectarianism. For this reason we began to preach these messages. Later God began to show us one by one the different truths, that is, the truths that we mentioned earlier. Gradually, we began to see the victory of Christ, the resurrection life, the teaching of the cross, the work of the Holy Spirit, and so forth. Everywhere in China men began to understand these things. In the course of our conversation with the Western missionaries, we discovered that many of these truths were also recovered in the same way in the West.

We know that God's truths are cumulative; later truths do not negate earlier ones. All the past truths of God form the foundation of the truths today. What we see today are the cumulative revelations of God. When God opens our eyes to see this fact, we begin to realize that we are living in the tide of God's will. This tide is a continuation of all the past works of God in previous ages.

From 1926 on, we began to release many messages concerning salvation, the church, and the cross, and we testified much concerning these things. By 1927 we concentrated our attention on the subjective work of the cross. We saw that concerning the cross, there is not only the truth concerning Christ's death, but there is also the fact of resurrection. In the past the resurrection which we preached was mainly a matter of faith; it was not related to our experience. What we speak of today is resurrection as a principle of life. It is not just a doctrine but a spiritual fact. It is like a grain of wheat that dies and brings forth many grains; it is the principle of resurrection. After this, God showed us what the Body of Christ is and where the reality of this Body is. We began to realize that as there is only one life of Christ, there is only one church.

Personally, I received much help from Mrs. Penn-Lewis. In England Mr. Austin-Sparks also received much help from her. Brother Sparks was a pastor in a Baptist chapel in southeast London. Later the Lord showed him different truths concerning the meaning of resurrection and the meaning of the church life.

We cannot say that the aforementioned truths did not exist before today. However, they have not been revealed as clearly as today. In spite of this, prior to 1928, we did not mention anything concerning the central matters of God. By February of 1928, we began to mention something concerning God's eternal purpose. From that time on, we began to tell people what God's eternal purpose is. In that year, we had our first Overcomer Conference. Afterward, we had a second Overcomer Conference. All of the things mentioned in these conferences were matters related to God's central theme.

Despite the above revelations, it was not until 1934 that we realized that the centrality of everything related to God is Christ. Christ is God's centrality and God's universality. All of God's plan is related to Christ. This is the truth that God is pleased to reveal to us in these days. It is also the message we are preaching during this conference. This is what God showed Brother Sparks also. He saw much of the truth concerning God's overcomers.

God's overcomers are a group of people who take the lead to

stand in the place of death on behalf of the whole congregation. Their relationship with the church is that of Zion's relationship with Jerusalem. All of God's requirements fall upon Zion. When Zion is gained, Jerusalem is gained. When both Zion and Jerusalem are secured, God's purpose is fulfilled.

Our hearts are full of thanksgiving to God. From all these brothers we have received much help. As Paul said, "Neither did I receive it from man" (Gal. 1:12). In the same way, we can say that although we have received help from our brothers, these revelations were not received from man. We received help from Luther, Zinzendorf, the Moravian Brethren, and the Keswick messages. Today we believe that God's ultimate goal is to have Christ as everything. One elderly pastor, Dr. F. B. Meyer, also saw this matter. However, by then he was already over ninety years old and could not do much work. I believe that God has only one work today. It is the message of Colossians 1:18 which says that God desires to see Christ have the first place in all things. The basis of everything is the death, the resurrection, and the ascension of Christ. Other than Christ, there is no spiritual reality. This is God's "present truth."

SOUNDING OUT A CALL

Hence, what are we doing today? We should answer as John the Baptist did that we are a voice in the wilderness (John 1:23). Our work is to sound out the call to God's children to return to God's central purpose, to take Christ as the center of all things, and to take His death, resurrection, and ascension as the basis of everything. This is the message of Colossians 1 and 3. We know the position of the church in the New Testament. We realize that this position is lofty and spiritual. We thank God for the help rendered to us from the Western missionaries. Yet God is showing us today that we should bring everything back to God's central purpose. Our work today is to return to the biblical ground of the church.

All of God's truth has the church as the starting point. Paul was first put in the church in Antioch. Later he was sent out from the church in Antioch. All of the truths that we preach today have the church as the starting point. This is our work and this is our testimony.

We should mention the miscellaneous truths less. We should do everything we can to show people that the Lord is the Head over all things. We are not here disrupting churches. Rather, we are here returning to the initial work of the apostles. We have to be careful about everything that we do. Everything that is of man we must learn to reject, and everything that is of God we must strive to attain.

We thank God that we can touch God's grand purpose. We need to humble and prostrate ourselves and to deny ourselves. We need to be clear that our work today is not just to save some souls or to help others become spiritual. Our goal is indeed the greatest and the most glorious. Thank God that we can know God's "present truth." May God be gracious to us so that we do not become the castaways of the "present truth." May we be watchful, and may we not allow the flesh to come in or the self to gain any ground. May God's will be accomplished in us.

FOUR RESPONSIBILITIES TODAY

Finally, I would like to add a few words. We have four responsibilities today: (1) Concerning the sinners, we have to preach the gospel. (2) Concerning Satan, we have to realize there is a spiritual warfare. (3) Concerning the church, we have to hold fast what we see today. (4) Concerning Christ, we should testify of the fact of His preeminence in all things. Today this testimony can be found in America, England, France, Spain, Africa, and everywhere. However, the number is not great. Outwardly speaking, their condition is also very poor. We should pray for these places. ❦

8

QUESTIONS RELATED TO THE WORKERS

"Now there were in Antioch, in the local church,
prophets and teachers: Barnabas and Simeon,
who was called Niger, and
Lucius the Cyrenian, and Manaen,
the foster brother of Herod the tetrarch, and Saul."
Acts 13:1

THE RAISING UP OF THE WORKERS

The first thing we want to see is how the workers are raised up. There are mainly two aspects in the raising up of the workers. The first involves localities where there are already meetings. If some brothers in a locality where meetings have started are burdened to go to another locality to work, they must be responsible before the Lord and also have the approval of all the brothers and sisters in the locality where they meet. This situation is like a finger wanting to move; the finger cannot move independently but must be carried along by the move of the whole body. It can only move after it has the approval of the whole body. Christ is the Head of the church. Therefore, the church is the Body of Christ. In a locality where there is no meeting, the Body is not manifested. In that case, an individual is responsible to God alone. But whenever a meeting is raised up in a locality, there is a need for the approval of the brothers and sisters. This can be seen from the record of

Acts 13. A meeting was started in Antioch, and the Holy Spirit through the Body sent Paul and Barnabas out to work.

Second, in a locality where there is not yet a meeting, the situation is different. If someone wants to work in a locality where there is no meeting, he has to be responsible to the Lord directly. In Acts 11, the church in Antioch had not yet appeared, so Paul and Barnabas were responsible to God directly. But later when the church was produced, the Holy Spirit sent out the prophets and teachers through the Body. By then the work of Paul and Barnabas was no longer just before God but was in the Body as well. The disciples laid hands on Paul and Barnabas and sent them out. The laying on of hands signifies sympathy and union. Through the laying on of hands, all the brothers were joined to Paul and Barnabas in their going out. The going of the two became the going of the whole Body. The laying on of hands is different from the ordination of pastors. The ordination practices we see today are traditions and are not found in the Bible.

After Paul and Barnabas were sent out from Antioch, they engaged themselves in the work commissioned by the Holy Spirit. This is the first case in history of missionary work. In this sending, the Holy Spirit maintained His absolute authority. A church cannot send out anyone on its own. Before the church can send, there must first be the speaking of the Holy Spirit. The sending of the church is merely the execution of the order of the Holy Spirit and the confirmation of the move of the Holy Spirit.

Acts 15:36-40 mentions another case of going out. In these verses we see the paths of Paul and Barnabas separating. Paul suggested that only two should go, but Barnabas insisted that they bring Mark along. Paul considered it unsuitable for Mark to join them. Between the two there was a sharp contention. Therefore, Barnabas decided to take Mark with him, but Paul chose Silas and took another way. Verse 40 says, "But Paul...went out, having been commended to the grace of the Lord by the brothers." This is the difference between the two men. Paul was sent out by the Body, while Barnabas did not have the sending of the Body. Paul was commended to the grace of the Lord by the brothers. Barnabas was not. In this matter, the Body stood on Paul's side. After Acts 15, Barnabas was not mentioned anymore. In this matter, the Holy Spirit confirmed the sending of the Body.

Mark played a passive role here. He was a young co-worker and learner. Therefore, he did not bear as great a responsibility as Barnabas. Later Mark was recovered by God and brought back into the work. But what about Barnabas? There was no return for him and no further mention of him. Some may ask, "Since that brother can do something, can I not do the same? Since that brother can go to a certain locality, can I not go to the same locality?" You have to be careful. That brother may go under the sending of the Body, while you might be going by yourself. This is where the difference lies. Do not say, "If God can use him, He can also use me." God can use him and not you, because he is sent out in the Body. Do not say that God cannot drop you; He can drop you in the same way that He dropped Barnabas. The record in Acts is very clear. After that incident, the Holy Spirit did not mention Barnabas again.

All the work may be done by individuals, but it is all done in the move of the Body. This was the case on the day of Pentecost. Acts 2:14 says, "But Peter, standing with the eleven, lifted up his voice and spoke forth to them." The word "standing" here is plural, while "lifted" is singular. Although one man was speaking, eleven others were standing behind this one. Therefore, we have to see that in our working, we must have the brothers behind us to be our support.

We need to learn the lesson of submission. Not only do the sent ones need to learn submission, the sending ones also need to learn submission. Only in the spirit of submission will a person hear the voice of the Holy Spirit. We cannot consider that a consensus is the standard for any work; rather, submission must be the standard. We should not send out a brother because we agree with him. Many times, even though we do not agree with the proposal of a certain brother, we still have to give him the liberty to do it. The matter is not about agreeing or not agreeing but about submitting or not submitting. The Holy Spirit can have a way only among the submissive ones.

Once a worker is sent out, he becomes an apostle. An apostle is a sent worker. Paul was an apostle. What is the difference between an apostle and an elder? According to the Bible, elders are stationary, while the apostles move. The elders are appointed for one locality only, while the apostles are for the whole Body. Paul was never an elder; he was only an apostle. But Peter and John were elders as well as apostles. When they were in Jerusalem, they were the elders in Jerusalem. In addition to being the elders in Jerusalem, they were also apostles. Because they were the elders, they had the authority to oversee. As to apostles, their responsibility is limited to only the work they are commissioned to do; they have no overseeing responsibility. I hope that we all will be clear. When speaking of the elders, it is with reference to one locality. When speaking of the apostles, it is with reference to the whole earth. The same person can have two statuses at the same time; on the one hand, he bears the overseeing responsibility in a locality, and on the other hand, he bears the responsibility of the work in all the localities. For example, among the brothers my work is for all the workers in all the localities, as well as for those in Shanghai. I share the responsibility in Shanghai with the brothers here.

THE RECOGNITION OF THE WORKERS

Now we will consider the workers. How do we recognize whether or not a person is a worker?

(1) A worker must have gifts. There are many kinds of gifts. Evangelism is a gift. Prophesying is a gift. Shepherding and teaching is also a gift. Different gifts are for different functions. The gift of the evangelists is for unbelievers. The gift of the teachers is for ascertaining doctrines. The gift of the shepherds is for shepherding men, nurturing believers for their spiritual growth, and rendering help for the solution of personal problems and different matters.

A worker should have as many of these gifts as possible. However, he must have at least one of these gifts.

How can we tell if a person has a certain gift? If he has a gift, the brothers who are meeting with him should be able to testify and confirm this. Therefore, the recognition of a gift is in the Body. The Body knows. If a person has the gift of an evangelist, the Body can sense it. If he has the gift of teaching, the Body can also sense it. Even if he does not take preaching as a profession, he can still have these gifts and do the work that the workers are doing. These gifts are what the workers should have, but they are not limited just to the workers.

Many people think that if they cannot work in one locality, they can change to another locality and perhaps work there. Actually, inability to work in a locality is not a matter of the locality. If someone cannot work in one locality, neither can he work in another locality. The question is whether or not he has a gift. A person who does not have a gift will not have a gift wherever he goes.

(2) Although a worker may have the gifts, if his life is not proper, he still cannot work. His work depends not only on the gift but also on the grace. He must not only have sufficient gifts but also an abundance of grace. The result of a work is not only related to the gift of the worker but also is directly related to the life of the worker. Workers with different amounts of grace will have different results in the same work. The amount of grace a worker has determines the kind of work that he produces. This does not mean that one who has no grace cannot bring others to salvation. Perhaps he can bring others to salvation because he has the gift of evangelism. But if he does not have life, the more work he does, the more tearing down there will be. Today many workers are building their work with one hand and tearing it down with the other hand because there is a lack of life.

In Acts 16:2 all the brothers commended Timothy. As a result, verse 3 tells us that Paul took Timothy with him. This is the confirmation of the brothers. Timothy was confirmed not only in one place by the brothers but in at least two places. If one's condition before the Lord is proper and the grace is adequate, the brothers who are meeting in the same locality will surely testify for him. Not only will spiritual brothers testify for him, even brothers who are not spiritual will also testify for him.

THE RELATIONSHIP BETWEEN THE WORKERS, THE MEETINGS, AND THE POSITION OF THE WORKERS

According to the Bible, every meeting should have three kinds of people. First, there are believers in the church. This is the basic group in a meeting. There is, at least, this first kind in every church. Second, there are those who serve in the material things. All of their responsibilities relate to business affairs, such as helping the brothers and sisters to do things, managing the arrangement and affairs concerning the meeting, etc. The Bible calls these people deacons, of whom some are brothers and some are sisters. Third, in addition to the above two kinds, there are a few brothers whose responsibilities are to take care of the main activities in the meetings, such as taking the lead in the meetings, making decisions, corresponding with those outside the church, and caring for the saints. The Bible calls these people elders.

A meeting should involve all of the above three types of people. There are no workers. Workers do not occupy a superior position in the church. Since a worker does not belong to another group of people, he must be in one of the above three groups. The workers do not become a fourth group in a meeting; they are within one of the other three.

The relationship among these three groups of people can be illustrated by an example. Suppose the brothers in a certain locality need to build a meeting hall. In the beginning, the elders make a proposal and decisions. After the matter has been decided, they will inform the brothers and assign various responsibilities to the deacons. The deacons, in turn, will ask all the brothers and sisters to provide the necessary labor. The workers can only do their share of the work. They can only fulfill their part of the work; they cannot control the whole work. The only difference between them and the other believers is that they bear a little more burden. This is the relationship between the workers and the local churches.

The position of the workers is similar to the position of the early apostles. They do the work of the apostles, but they do not have the authority of the apostles. On the other hand, if a worker has a certain commission, burden, or assignment from the Lord, the church should show its sympathy in the matter and support his endeavors. We cannot find one example in the Bible where the apostles had a burden and the church did not agree with it or where the work was under the control of a church. If this is the case, God's work will be greatly hindered.

THE RELATIONSHIP BETWEEN THE YOUNGER WORKERS AND OLDER WORKERS

What is the relationship between the younger workers and the older workers in the work? According to the Bible, the workers who come afterward should submit to the workers who were there before them. The younger should submit to the older. For example, Paul was clearly leading Silas, Timothy, Titus, and Onesimus. The younger ones were clearly taking Paul's leading and were submissive to Paul.

Today in the denominations, there are two situations. On the one hand, some workers are completely controlled and bound by those above them, and all of the decisions arise from human ideas. At the other extreme, there are the so-called free-lance preachers. They come and go independently; they provide for themselves and do their preaching. They are not bound or controlled by anyone. However, neither kinds of people know the Lord. The first group places authority in the hands of others; they do not have the Lord. The second group keeps the authority in their own hand; they also do not have the Lord. When the authority is placed in the Lord's hand, these two extremes are crossed out. A worker must not be controlled by others in the matter of money and must not hand this authority over to others.

Acts 8 tells us that Peter and John were sent by the church to preach in Samaria. Their footsteps were restricted by the church. Every worker is a restricted person. Many people think that they are under the control of no one. They are misled to think that a spiritual person is without restriction.

Concerning the perfecting of the young ones, the Bible does

not speak of any seminary. Although some tried to start a school for the prophets in the Old Testament, it did not produce any prophets. Studying in a seminary will not make a person a worker. The training of a worker comes from following a pattern and from submission.

Timothy and Silas both followed Paul. In the Bible, we only see the way of apprenticeship; we do not see the way of scholarship. If a young worker does not learn the lesson of submission properly, he will not be able to learn any other lesson. This is something very important. Every young worker must go through great pressure in the hand of God before he can become useful. Everyone used by God has had to pass through strict dealings. One can see from the letter Paul wrote to Timothy that he was very strict in his instructions to the younger workers. He was not at all careless or loose with Timothy.

THE PREACHING OF THE YOUNG WORKERS

Many of the problems in the church today arise when men want to have the gifts but do not get them. They think that they are a certain kind of gift, but actually they are not. When matters are put into their hands, they spoil them. This does not mean that they do not want to handle the matters properly. It merely means that they do not have the capacity to handle them properly. A person with the gift of teaching can only do the work of discerning biblical truths, maintaining these truths, and discovering new truths; he cannot do anything else. Similarly, those who only have the gift of evangelism can only do the work of evangelism; they cannot replace the teachers to teach and ascertain the truth. They can only do the work within their limit. The problem is that no one in the world today is keeping to his own position or is satisfied with his own position. The evangelists want to be the teachers, while the teachers want to be evangelists. Everyone admires what they are not. This tendency of the natural man is the flesh. In the Body of Christ, every member has its distinct use. The ear cannot replace the eye, and the eye cannot replace the ear. Even if you put the ear in the position of the eye, the ear is still the ear; it still cannot see. This shows us the importance of standing firm in our position. Everyone of us has to learn to stand in our own position.

The younger workers must not only submit to the older workers personally but must also know where God has put them. After one understands his proper position, he will not fall into the flesh. In this way, he will experience deliverance in his work. If a young worker indeed has the gift of teaching and the older workers around him do not have this gift, in this circumstance, the older ones should submit to the younger one and receive his gift. However, every younger worker can always find someone who is more mature and more advanced from whom he can learn submission. There will always be some older workers to whom he can submit. Timothy was charged to consider what Paul said (2 Tim. 2:7) and know "from which ones you have learned them" (2 Tim. 3:14). Timothy had to go and find the ones from whom he had learned all the things. He had to find the workers who were ahead of him.

A young worker must also learn to accept unreasonable treatment. He must learn what it means to submit without reason. All true submission is without reason. Once there is a reason, it is not submission. In God's work, no one can be independent and claim that he does not need to submit to anyone else. The younger ones should be this way and even the older ones are without an exception because no one can be independent. Even if God uses a worker to discover a certain truth, he cannot move independently; he must go on in mutual submission.

THE FAITH OF THE WORKERS

All of the workers must have the common faith concerning the Lord's work and His person. These basic truths must be kept in common by us. If any worker has erred in these general principles, the elders should stop him from working. Concerning the major doctrines, there must be the proper scriptural interpretations. Everyone must be the same in these interpretations. The proper interpretation of many verses have already been laid down by others. All we have to do is receive them from their hand; there is no need for us to add anything. One basic principle in reading the Bible is to simply accept what God's Word says and not add our own thoughts to it. In reading the Bible, we should ask, "What has God said?" instead of "Why did God say this?" A citizen of a country does not need to ask why there is a certain law. He only needs to ask what the law of the country is. Our question should be "what," not "why." Our attitude toward God's commands should not be one of understanding but of submission.

Today, due to differences in men's conduct before God, there are differences in biblical interpretations. For example, in the matter of baptism, many people have been sprinkled. When they read the Bible, they somehow find the doctrine of sprinkling. Their doctrine is a result of their conduct. A man's interpretation of the Bible has a great deal to do with his attitude before God. Many people come to God's Word with only one purpose: to find an ordinance that would justify their conduct. Their goal is to turn God's Word into some law that suits them. Therefore, their interpretation of the Bible is all for themselves. A person who has never passed through the dealing of the cross cannot read the Bible. Only those who have passed through the cross can read the Bible properly.

THE NEED OF THE WORKERS

Now we come to the need of the workers. The first thing we have to mention is the offering of money by the believers. The offerings of the believers are not merely for the support of the workers; they are to supply those who work for the Lord. In other words, one does not offer to a certain person simply because he is a worker; he offers to that person because he works for the Lord. What he is personally is one matter, and whether or not he works is another matter altogether. As long as he works for the Lord, he deserves to be supplied. The question is not whether or not he has money, but whether or not he works for the Lord. If he works for the Lord, he deserves to be supported. A man paying a rickshaw operator does not ask if he is rich or poor. Whether he is rich or poor has nothing to do with it. As long as he has worked, he deserves his wages. A person cannot say that because a worker has money, he does not need to be supported. Someone once intended to make an offering to Mr. Bright, a co-worker of Dr. Scofield. But the person next to him said that the Lord would take care of Mr. Bright's needs. Therefore, the man took back his offering, and Mr. Bright was left without the support. Believers should not offer their money just because the workers are poor. If they give because of the worker's poverty, they are not making an offering but are giving alms.

Making an offering is the least that a saved person can do. If a saved man does not offer up himself, he is a useless person before God. If a man has received grace, there should be a result of offering up all that he has to the Lord. It is not normal for a person to receive grace and not be willing to offer up all that he has. All those whose hearts have been touched by God will give up their money purse. It is impossible for a person's heart to be touched by God without his possessions also being touched by God. Consecration allows God to touch everything. Only after God has touched him will love flow out from him. If a man has never offered up himself, there will surely not be the outflow of love from him.

Today, there are only two gods in this world. The first is mammon, and the other is the true God. If we do not love God, we will love mammon. Only when a man loves God will his heart be broadened. The thing that broadens man's heart the most is the giving of money. A believer among us attended meetings in a certain denomination for twenty years but never even nodded his head toward another person. Later he offered himself up, and his whole being changed. Previously I was afraid of reporting to others about our financial condition. But today I have turned. This is a way for others to receive grace. The more a person offers, the more he will be filled with grace. These words are for the whole Body.

Now let us consider the way to dispense the offerings. Part of the money received in the meetings should be set aside for the local workers and the workers in other localities. This is a sign of fellowship. Paul praised the Philippians for their grace in this matter (Phil. 4). They continued to fellowship with the apostle in the matter of money. The condition of the Corinthians was just the opposite; they developed a problem in their fellowship with Paul. As a result, Paul was willing to allow other churches to suffer, rather than ask for any money from the Corinthians. He did not use the Corinthians' money because there was a problem with the fellowship. Only when there is fellowship can there be a material offering.

Thank the Lord that the brothers in Shanghai have received grace in this matter. The workers from out of town should not misunderstand and think that the church in Shanghai is so rich that it can keep sending money out. The reason the church in Shanghai is able to send money out is because the local workers in Shanghai have received only a little local support. Thus, the church is able to send out so much. This is the grace of the church in Shanghai.

The offerings to individuals should be personally wrapped in an envelope by the offerer, marked with the name of the worker, and dropped into the offering box. The brothers who open the box should then personally hand this offering directly to the receiver.

THE WAY THE WORKERS HANDLE THEIR FINANCES

First, workers should not make others feel that they are poor. A worker lives by faith, not by alms giving. It is a shame to let others know that you are poor with the hope of receiving support. When a worker receives a supply from the brothers, he should have the proper attitude. When a worker receives money from the brothers, he is receiving this money on God's behalf. He stands on God's side and represents God. Therefore, he should not have a beggarly attitude. When Paul mentioned the matter of money, he gave others an honorable and respectable impression. This is the proper attitude for every worker.

Second, whenever any worker receives more than other workers, he should distribute the excess to the other workers. Do not be afraid that by doing this, others will misunderstand and think that you are rich or have struck a fortune. Moreover, for personal family needs, there is sometimes the necessity of short-term savings. This is scriptural. Proverbs teaches this.

Third, there must be some planning in the way one uses his money. Many people buy useless things when they have money. This kind of behavior will stop God's supply. One has to plan the way he uses his money. One must have a budget and carefully consider before God what he should and should not buy. He should not buy carelessly and waste money.

Fourth, workers must never borrow. A worker of God should prefer to die than borrow from others. If he does not have the faith that his living will be cared for, he should look for some work to sustain his living. If he has the faith that God will sustain him, he should not stretch out his hand to others.

THE PRINCIPLE OF MANNA

Today, God desires that we walk according to the principle of manna. The principle of manna is: "He who gathered much had no excess, and he who gathered little had no lack" (2 Cor. 8:15). This is not just the record in the Old Testament. The New Testament tells us the same thing. Being in excess and being in want are both wrong. If a brother in a locality cannot get by and has no means to support his living, either the church or individual believers should help him. The church cannot sit there and do nothing for the brothers who are unemployed; it must do its best to help them. Of course, this does not include those who will not work. We cannot help those who are not willing to work. We can only help those who are willing to work. Moreover, if the earning of a brother is not enough to support his living, the church must again come in to help. The same is true with those whose income is too low. It was this kind of work that the apostles did in the early church.

The order for helping is to care for the brothers and sisters in your locality first, and then to help the poor people outside. If believers have close family members who have needs, they should care for the needs of their own relatives first, before caring for the needs of other people.

No one should give offerings without first having some careful consideration. A naturally loose person will not receive the Lord's blessing through excessive giving, because a person who is loose with his finances will surely be loose in the things of the Lord. We have to learn to be a consecrated person before the Lord, not a loose person.

For a believer, giving is not a matter of simply offering money. One must have a proper living before God before his giving can receive God's blessing. The third Epistle of John mentions that the saints who support the workers need to have a living worthy of God and one that is in a godly manner. A person who gives must live a life that is worthy of God. Thank the Lord that everyone is not a Lazarus, and everyone is not a rich man. God does not need Lazarus, nor does He need the rich man. He only needs the offerings of those whose living is worthy of Him. Although Lazarus did not have money, he could be saved; he could receive grace and live a life worthy of God. The flesh has two sins before God. One is the severe treatment of the body mentioned in Colossians 2. The other is to indulge oneself in comfort. God has no intention for us to treat our body severely, but neither does He want us to live too comfortably. He wants us to live a life that is worthy of Him. All excess money should be given away as quickly as possible.

THE LETTER OF RECOMMENDATION

The last thing to mention is the letter of recommendation. Paul mentioned this to the Corinthians. This is something found in the New Testament. When an ordinary believer goes to a new locality, he should have a letter of recommendation. Paul mentioned in his Epistle that he himself did not need a letter of recommendation. This is because Paul had already built up a relationship with the

Corinthians. This is why he was an exception. As to the other brothers and sisters, a letter of recommendation was still necessary. The function of the letter is twofold. First, it allows others to know you. Second, it prevents false brothers from coming in. Every letter of recommendation should be witnessed by two or three persons before it can be validated. Usually a letter of recommendation is written by the local elders or the responsible persons. There are three kinds of letters:

(1) Those that recommend a brother to the Lord's table, attesting that he is a brother in the Lord. This is mainly for the brothers who are still in the denominations.

(2) Those that recommend that a brother has left the denominations and is taking the way we take.

(3) In addition to those taking this way, there are those who have special gifts and can be invited to speak.

After receiving a letter of recommendation, the local responsible ones should send a letter of reply to the sending locality, verifying that the letter of recommendation was received. Such letters of recommendation and replies should be prepared ahead of time and printed according to a standard form, so that they can be used easily. Every time a brother comes from another locality, he needs to give us a letter of recommendation before we can receive him at the Lord's table. We will likewise furnish those who go out from us with a letter of recommendation. I hope that we all will pay attention to this matter in the future. ✱